The Desires Of Thine Heart

The Desires Of Thine Heart

Felecia Berry LMSW

Library of Congress Control Number: 2011962777
ISBN: Hardcover   978-1-4691-3836-7
                 Softcover   978-1-4691-3835-0
                 Ebook   978-1-4691-3837-4

Copyedited and indexed by Vicente Raphael Bandillo
Reviewed by Janeth Parreño

All scripture quotations are from the King James and NIV Version of the Bible.

This book was printed in the United States of America.

To order additional copies of this book, contact:
Xlibris Corporation
1-888-795-4274
www.Xlibris.com
Orders@Xlibris.com

There is no greater agony than
bearing an untold story inside you.

~ Dr. Maya Angelou

To Jesus Christ my Lord and Savior for giving me the Desires of My Heart. To my mother, Beverly Berry, my sister Christine Hill, and God's sweetest blessing to me, Samuel

CONTENTS

FORWARD

Everyone has a story. When women get together, we love to tell our stories about how we grew up, about our moms and dads, about love and life. If you care to listen, you will hear all about childbirth, about each of our children, about our family and friends, about taking care of our parents in their later years, and about our losses. Our stories are filled with joys and sorrows, defeats and victories. Those who listen validate our feelings and experiences. Those who listen "bless" us by honoring our "voice," allowing us the freedom to share in our own words, in our own fashion of storytelling.

Felecia Berry is about to tell you her story. A Scripture came to my mind as I read her book for the first time. Second Corinthians 1:3 says, "Praise to the God and Father of our Lord Jesus Christ, the Father of compassion and the God of all comfort, who comforts us in all our troubles, so that we can comfort those in any trouble with the comfort we ourselves have received from God" (NIV translation).

I am not surprised that Felecia is telling her story as a means of comforting and encouraging you. Her discovery for herself and her message to you is clear: "All you have to do is walk in your victory."

I met Felecia when she was a senior social-work student at Marygrove College, and at that time she was learning to walk in her victory. As her social-work field supervisor, I heard her story, and I praise God for this remarkable young woman who has found Christ to be her victory-giver in every circumstance of life. Her story will come alive for you because she has a passion to help others experience the same freedom and victory granted to her by our Loving Heavenly Father. She gives voice to the truth that in Christ, we are "free indeed" from every obstacle, hurt, and struggle in life, on the inside and out (John 8:34-36).

Felecia is a woman filled with dreams, empowered by the Spirit of the Living God. While she was a student, she exercised Christ's compassion by caring for the hungry and needy in Hamtramck, MI. It was her idea to start a food bank and to help those most vulnerable to food insecurity. Hamtramck Harvest (now known as Harvest House) was born as her senior project. Since late 1998, this ministry continues to bless hundreds of families each month with fresh produce, meat, and canned goods.

Do you have a dream? Do you believe that God has plans for you? Your story will unfold daily, by God's grace, if you have faith to believe in his deep, wide and awesome love for you. If you need encouragement on your journey, you will surely find it here.

~ Rev. Sharon A. Buttry, LMSW

Having been a grief counselor for over thirteen years, watching the emotional rollercoaster of grieving families, I find myself wondering why God allows us to be subjected to difficult and tragic life experiences. However, as a Pastor, I have come to understand that sometimes God takes us through seasons of purging before he reveals his reason and purpose for our lives.

Ms. Berry has identified the reason and has shown courage in baring her soul in the hope of helping others to heal. I am certain, because of her faithfulness; God will walk with her on this journey of healing and restoration. My prayer is that, through her story, you will experience healing as well.

~ Rev. Karen Gray Sheffield

PROLOGUE

In the spring of 1999, I was asked to deliver the message at the local church where my close friends were pastors. The message was to come from the book of Nehemiah. I was a little confused about what text or scripture within the book of Nehemiah I was expected to expound upon. So I posed this question to my pastor friend, and she told me, "The whole book."

"Expound on the whole book of Nehemiah?" I asked in amazement. "My friend was very firm on that score, very firm about the kind of message she wanted me to present that evening.

Because I did not have a lot of time to prepare the message, I solicited the help of my sister, Christine. Together we began to read the book of Nehemiah, and we were astounded by his plight to rebuild Jerusalem after the Babylonians destroyed it and sent the inhabitants into exile. I found Nehemiah's story so compelling because his tale of tragedy, rebuilding, and restoration was reminiscent of my life story. At the time, I was in a period of mental, physical, spiritual, and emotional restoration.

There was always a passion within me to help hurting and wounded people. This work, performed mainly in the nonprofit sector, does not pay hefty salaries, but its rewards are great because you are assisting individuals, families, and groups in putting the puzzle pieces of their lives back together after the worst has happened. As a helping professional, I always, always navigated to individuals who experienced mental, physical, emotional, and sexual trauma. Whenever duty calls, I am a "first responder" in aiding and assisting women, teens, and children affected by mental, physical, sexual, and emotional trauma. Yet, after my graduation from college, my passion, commitment, and focus were changing, and I was headed in a direction that would have created a great distance between me and the hurting individuals who would need me in order for them to achieve greater income and prominence in the community.

As I prepared for the message, I was in a good place spiritually *and* emotionally. I had recently graduated with my master's degree in social work from Wayne State University. My dreams and aspirations were to make some serious money as a professional social worker. I had a crazy dollar figure in my head. The jobs that would help me obtain my financial goals were at the state level or in for-profit hospitals. I was at a time in my life when I was embarking on a new chapter. I had sugar-plum visions of traveling to Africa to buy African clothing, jewelry, and artifacts to deck out a home I had not yet bought.

I had an inward desire to travel to warm, exotic destinations by land, air, and sea. I had a desire to go on shopping sprees in New York, Chicago, Los Angeles, and Paris. All on a master social worker's salary! I had survived the worst in my life, and now I was headed to a new frontier of total, self-absorbed bliss. My feelings were that this new frontier would recompense me for all my mental, physical, and emotional suffering. Yep, it was all about *me*!

My logic was that life had dealt me a bad hand, and, by God's grace, I had been able to turn the tide and head in a direction that would afford me everything I had missed along the way. I had two college degrees under my belt and several job offers on the table. I had stepped on my fear of failure and defeat and begun climbing the ladder of success and was just starting to reap its benefits.

I was having lunch with city leaders, bankers, business owners, program directors, authors, and community leaders. I was attending a meeting with a local judge who complimented me on my hair and attire and who whispered to a fellow judge, "She's got the look." I was sitting on planning committees with doctors and judges in the fight against domestic violence. I had met with local representatives and lawmakers in Lansing, Michigan, and city hall in Downtown Detroit. When I wrote a letter to my representative about a streetlight that did not work in my neighborhood, not only did the light get fixed but the repair person left a little note tacked on my front door indicating that the light was repaired.

During a crucial presidential election—they are all crucial—I played an active role in the voter-registration process (during which I made the startling revelation that many of my family members were not registered voters!). Oh yeah, in my mind, I was all that! Do not get me wrong, I did not become smug or uppity; I was just like a kid in "candy land," grinning and pinching myself along the way.

However, like Nehemiah, I had to go back and rescue some people who were still in the thicket of trauma and tragedy. I had to go back and pull women from the ruins of abusive relationships, depression, and low self-esteem. I had to go back to aid and assist them in restoring and rebuilding their lives. I had to go back and be the shoulder to cry on. I had to go back and be the shoulder to lean on. This, I know for sure, was what I was called to do. God had given me a reality check about my purpose and assignment on this earth, and that is to carry out his will, purpose, and saving of souls. I was sent to literally snatch souls out the fiery pit of hell for God's plan and his kingdom.

That night, the message I taught on Nehemiah would become the needed seed planted in me to fulfill my purpose and potential in life; only, I did not know it at the time. I can be special like that sometime.

The night I taught the message on Nehemiah, I allowed God to lead me because I was nervous about bringing a message to a group of people I had never met. Never before had I taught a message outside my home church. That night, my sister and I read and collaborated on what we had read and what we believed God was trying to convey to his people. I prayed beforehand and asked God to move me, Felecia, out of the way. This particular prayer always helps with the nervousness.

On the drive to the church, I thought no one would show up. When I arrived at the church, there were cars parked everywhere! There were cars on the street, cars parked in the church parking lot, cars parked down the street. It was a Friday night!

Once Christine and I arrived inside the church, I met with my friend, and she prepped me for the evening and reiterated the message. I asked if I could take a peek into the sanctuary, and she said yes. The sanctuary was filling up fast. I was filling up fast—with fear. I was thinking, *Maybe I cannot do this.* The devil will try you like that at critical moments when you are doing a good work for God. I was second-guessing myself. Like, maybe this is a mistake. My knees started knocking.

My sister read my facial expression. She's good at that. Without mentioning what she knew was going on inside my head, Christine gave me a stern look and said, "Let's pray." We prayed, right then and there. The devil was not going to get the victory. Not that night. God was doing something behind the scenes, and I had to show up for him to get the glory. It was not about me or how I felt. God had chosen me to bring an encouraging word to his people that night.

After the anointed prayer, I was ushered into the sanctuary, and I found that even *more* people were present now. I was nervous at first. My voice was shaky, and I was stumbling over my words. As an introduction and to settle down internally, I said a general prayer and began the message by reading the beginning of the chapter because I believed that was where God would have me to start.

1. The words or story of Nehemiah, son of Hacaliah: Now in the month of Chislev in the twentieth year [of the Persian King], as I was in the castle of the Shushan,

2. Hanani, one of my kinsmen, came with certain men from Judah, and I asked them about the surviving Jews who had escaped exile, and about Jerusalem.

3. And they said to me, "The remnant there in the province who escaped the exile are in great trouble and reproach; the wall of Jerusalem is broken down, and its [fortified] gates are destroyed by fire."

4. When I heard this, I sat down and wept and mourned for days and fasted and prayed [constantly] before the God of heaven. (Nehemiah 1:1–4 Amplified)

I began to expound on the text and got a few amen's, hallelujahs, and hand claps. The point I attempted to make was that, while I was in a good place and things were going well, there were sisters in the trenches battling and trying to come out of the cycle of abusive relationships, addictions, depressions, hopelessness, and helplessness. There were sisters masking the pain of their past with drugs, alcohol, multiple sex partners, and attempted suicides; and, thanks be to God, I was hand-selected by God to go back and pull them up and out with my testimony.

Then something changed; I began to compare the message to my personal life. I began to share my trials, my tragedies, and, finally, my victories. The congregation rose to its feet! The music ministry began striking chords; women were standing up, crying and shouting, clapping and dancing. I could not stop talking about how God brought me out of ruin to a place of triumph to reach back and help people rebuild their lives.

My prayer is that my story goes far beyond the walls of that church on that Friday night in the city of Detroit. The goal of my story is to tell the world that, what God did for me, he can do for you! It does not matter at what point you are in your life, God has a plan and promise for you!

The time has come to reach back and pull my sisters out of a continuous cycle of violence—of mental, physical, sexual, verbal, and emotional victimization perpetrated by their intimate partners. I believe the only way to approach the subject of moving forward after the worst happened is to share my story. My prayer is that my story will save, empower, and enlighten individuals who live, worship, and work among us every day.

I had God's seal of approval long before that church meeting. I had been preapproved for this calling long before I was formed in my mother's belly.

> 5 Before I formed thee in the belly, I knew thee; and, before thou camest forth out of the womb, I sanctified thee, and I ordained thee a prophet unto the nations.
>
> 6 Then I said, "Ah, Lord God! behold! I cannot speak for I am a child."
>
> 7 But the Lord said unto me, "Say not, 'I am a child': for thou shalt go to all that I shall send thee, and whatsoever I command thee thou shalt speak.
>
> 8 Be not afraid of their faces: for I am with thee to deliver thee," saith the Lord.
>
> 9 Then the Lord put forth his hand, and touched my mouth. And the Lord said unto me, "Behold, I have put my words in thy mouth.
>
> 10 See, I have this day set thee over the nations and over the kingdoms, to root out, and to pull down, and to destroy, and to throw down, to build and to plant." (Jeremiah 1:5–10)

CHAPTER 1

The Gathering

*The thief cometh not, but for to steal, and to kill and to destroy: I am come
that they might have life, and they might have it more abundantly.*

—John 10:10

THE DEATH OF my paternal grandmother, Mary Leslie Berry, in the
spring of 1989 marked a spiritual, mental, physical, and emotional milestone
in my life. As a child, my fondest memories of Grandma were of drinking
hot, percolated coffee with her in her sunny, bright yellow kitchen. The
smell of the hot coffee was intoxicating. Grandma sat perched on her
kitchen chair in front of a big black stove with the oven door open to
generate heat in her big kitchen. I cannot recall our exact ages but I believe
Christine, my younger sister, was five and I was seven years old. I like to
think of those moments as our "age of innocence" when all was right with
the world. We felt safe, loved, and protected. It was family time with our
beloved Grandma. Grandma, my sister, Christine, and I would sit around
the kitchen table sipping mugs of hot coffee, lost in our own thoughts while
more coffee brewed. Christine was so tiny. Her little legs dangled from her
chair as she sipped her coffee.

Wow, where did the time go? I can still remember the caramel taste of
the coffee. For years after, as a coffee drinker, I would ladle my coffee with
sugar and cream to get the taste I remembered in Grandma's kitchen, but,

for some reason, it just never tasted the same. It was a hit or miss. Sometimes it was pure frustration trying to capture the taste of that delicious coffee.

I had a tremendous revelation about my coffee dilemma in April of 2000 while attending a conference on grief and loss in Seattle, Washington, a state that knows a lot about coffee. I was walking to dinner with a conference attendee from Belize, and the subject of coffee came up. I shared with him how I could not get my coffee to taste like my grandmother's, and, as we kept walking, he looked at me and said, "The coffee does not taste the same because you miss your grandmother."

He continued to walk on, but I stopped in my tracks as the realization that I had been trying to capture the days of old in the sanctuary of Grandma's kitchen hit me, full force. Her kitchen was like the calm before the storm of the realities of life came into play. I missed those days of feeling loved unconditionally. I missed feeling safe and protected. I missed helping her wash dishes and then pouring a pot of hot scalding water on them to rinse them at the end. (I scald my dishes to this very day.) I missed her wet kisses on my cheek when I entered her home. I missed combing and brushing her long gray hair and oiling her scalp. I missed her belly- and knee-slapping laughs. I missed the days of her dropping those little sugar-substitute tablets into her coffee and mine (Grandma was diabetic). I missed those days of her exposing her plump thigh to give herself an insulin injection. Once, she asked me to give her a shot. I was scared out of my wits as she positioned her meaty thigh for the injection. I do not think I did too well because she never asked me to do that again.

In preparation for Grandma's funeral, several family members had flown into Detroit from Boston, Massachusetts, and Myrtle Beach, South Carolina. As I grieved my grandmother's death, I looked forward to seeing my beloved cousins after a long absence. At that time, the cousins' ages ranged from the mid-thirties to early forties. Time and distance had taken us in different directions over the course of the years.

That afternoon, after a round of hugs and kisses, we all congregated around my kitchen table. Like my grandmother, my house had a huge kitchen where everyone would gather during visits. Instead of rounds of hot coffee, we were drinking Captain Morgan Spiced Rum and Vernor's Ginger Ale. It was a workday. Ordinarily, I would not have been drinking at this time of day during the week, but I had taken a bereavement leave from my job.

At that time, I had a job I absolutely despised, working as a switchboard operator at a major bank in Downtown Detroit. Answering a switchboard at a major bank that experienced a high volume of calls was at times mentally and emotionally challenging. I was stuck in this job because I had failed to complete my college degree. I did not possess marketable skills; as a result, I qualified only for entry-level jobs, and the switchboard position fell into that category. It was not the job I wanted; it was the job I needed to sustain myself economically. Now I take total blame and responsibility for the actions that led me to that point in my life. I had made a series of bad choices and decisions.

Alcoholism was generational in our family, and many of us were heavy substance abusers as a result. Sadly, some of us were following in the substance-abuse footsteps of our fathers. It was all we ever talked about— our fathers and their alcoholism and mental illness. As adults, we had learned about the family's obsession with alcohol but never knew *why*. We never learned the root causes of our fathers' addiction to alcohol; we only saw the effects. My grandmother buried four sons prior to her death. I saw her cry a lot. It was heartbreaking for me, as a kid, to attend those funerals of my uncles.

As my cousins and I sat around the kitchen table chatting, laughing, reminiscing, and drinking to mask the sorrow of losing Grandma, one of my cousins, who was standing near the kitchen pantry door, holding a glass of Captain Morgan Spiced Rum in his hand, said, "We are never going to amount to anything. Just look at us; we are all in our thirties and forties. This is it; this is all there is. We are all too old to become anything greater than what we are now. It's too late for us to start over in life. It's too late to begin again. It's over." And with this seemingly life-changing proclamation that we were all destined for failure, he hung his head. At first, it seemed as if we were all in agreement; the kitchen fell into a dead silence. His stinging words—stifling and suffocating—hung in the air. No one, not one person, uttered a single word to counteract his statement.

After what seemed like an eternity, I mustered up the strength, through the lump in my throat, and—with slurred speech—to say, "No, that's not true. There is more to life. We're just not living it." At that point, everyone chimed in to disagree with his statement. Still, his daunting words had taken hold of me. I held fast to them. I knew I had to come up with a game plan because failure was not an option for me. No one had to tell me that I was not living life to the fullest. All I had to do was look around at my friends and family members who were striving, sacrificing, and making great strides in their personal lives and professional careers. They were traveling, getting promotions, getting married, starting businesses, buying homes, leasing apartments, and driving decent cars—and, lastly, they were not sitting around the kitchen table drinking away their troubles with us that afternoon.

Yes, I knew better. Hindsight is twenty-twenty; sometimes you have be careful of the company you are keeping because some companions, including friends and family, will try to keep you down in the barrow of crabs with them. Sadly, some people have no dreams, desires, goals, or aspirations in life; and you offend them with your giddy hopes, dreams, and aspirations to become something greater than what you are by tapping into your God-given talents. You become a threat to them because you expose their fear that they will never reach or that they have failed to reach their full potential because they are too lazy to go through the process and sacrifice it takes to attain one's goals, dreams, and aspirations.

True enough, we each had mental, physical, and emotional battle scars and blows from life's trials, and some of us held a jaded outlook on life after experiencing those trials and finding ourselves in straitened circumstances, but was throwing in the towel the only option? Something inside of me would not quit or give into my cousin's outlook for my future. I had taken up a fighting stance on many occasions during a storm, and I compared myself to a balloon that you punch and punch but which always bounces back. To me, this was just another punch from which I had to bounce back.

My cousin's crass statement that we would never become what God predestined us to be was a defining moment for me—causing me to come out of the rut of depression, self-loathing, risqué behavior, and low self-esteem I had been in. From that very moment, I was on a personal mission: I had to let the past go! I had to let the negative influences go! I was determined to break the mind-set that gave up on all that life had to offer mentally, spiritually, physically, financially, and emotionally. Sitting in the kitchen was a long way from sitting in the warmth of Grandma's kitchen. The harsh reality of life had set in, and I was on a mission to get my life back.

After my grandmother's funeral, my cousins packed up their belongings and headed home. I waved goodbye to them as they drove away. I was determined to change the course of my life. I was going to rewrite my story. I was not going to let my cousin's seed of discouragement take root in my life. Giving up was not an option. My life was not over. Yes, I had hit a few speed bumps, but I still had life in me. I was determined to finish what I had started as far as college was concerned. It did not happen overnight. I was still in a mental, physical, and abusive relationship with my boyfriend. I was still working as a switchboard operator. I was drinking heavily, but

I was determined to move forward. My cousin's proclamation to give up propelled me to walk forward. I received a wake-up call to rouse me from my state of just sitting and waiting for something great to happen but doing nothing to get the process started. This impromptu cocktail hour was the kick in the pants that I needed to finally get motivated and inspired to change my direction in life.

For years I had been sitting at a gate contemplating my next move. Like the story of the four leprous men in 2 Kings 7:3–6:

> 3-And there were four leprous men at the entering in of the gate: and they said one to another, "Why sit we here until we die?
>
> 4- If we say, 'We will enter into the city,' then the famine is in the city, and we shall die there: and if we sit still here, we die also. Now therefore come, and let us fall unto the host of the Syrians: and if they save us alive, we shall live; and if they kill us, we shall but die."
>
> 5- And they rose up in the twilight, to go unto the camp of the Syrians: and when they were come to the uttermost part of the camp of Syria, behold, there was no man there.
>
> 6- For the Lord had made the host of the Syrians to hear a noise of chariots, and a noise of horses, even the noise of a great host: and they said one to another, "Lo, the King of Israel hath hired against us the kings of the Hitties, and the Kings of the Egyptians, to come upon us."

Like the lepers, I was sitting at a gate of decision. They made a decision to either die in their present condition and circumstances or move forward, not knowing what was ahead. Once they made the decision to move forward, God had already worked the situation out for them. Because the four lepers took a leap of faith; they walked into blessings beyond measure. However, they first had to stop wallowing in self-pity and dwelling on missed opportunities and past failures and press forward. Sitting at that kitchen table was my hour of decision. I was wounded emotionally, bruised physically, and struggling mentally; the devil wanted me to believe I was unwanted and unloved and that I was a social outcast destined to live a life of self-destruction and defeat. The devil wanted me to die in my present state, yet God had a plan for me on the other side of the gate. Everything I needed was prepared for me, but I had to get off my "behind" and walk toward it. Determined not to die in my present condition, I set out to move forward. I knew what was behind me: hurt, pain, rejection, abandonment, and anguish. My present condition looked dismal; and I could have believed my cousin's prognosis that my life was over at thirty-something, but God had a master plan for me.

After my cousins' departure, I picked up a Bible and began thumbing through it. Over the years, I had rarely looked at a Bible; thankfully, there was one in the house. I was not active in the church. I could not remember the last time I had attended. I sat down at the same kitchen table where I'd hosted the Captain Morgan cocktail hour days earlier and began to thumb through the book, not knowing where to begin.

The Holy Spirit was beckoning me to come just as I was in my state of brokenness. I believed God was angry with me for my lifestyle. I had a potty-mouth; I was hateful and angry a lot. I wanted to clean up my act before I went to church and gave my life to Christ. I was under the impression that I needed to pull myself together before I came to God. Yet, as I fumbled through the Bible and searched the scriptures, I was hungering for more. I was trying with all my heart to understand what was written in the scriptures. It was as if the spirit of the Lord was in the kitchen prompting me to keep reading and searching for the real truth of his love for me.

As I sat reading the Bible, I knew I earnestly wanted to fill the void in my life. I had tried drugs, partying, boyfriends, and alcohol; these vices were only masking my inner pain. It was a sort-of Band-Aid effect. The drugs, alcohol, boyfriends, and parties were temporary solutions to try to cover up long-standing problems. Over the years, I had lost my faith in God. I was in a state of disconnect. I did not pray, attend church, or seek fellowship with God. I blamed God for all my shortcomings. I blamed God for taking my father at an early age. I blamed God for my traumatic childhood. I blamed God for the rape. I blamed God for the abusive relationship. I screamed and cursed God. In a state of mental anguish, I ripped a cross from the wall and stomped on it. I blamed God because I lacked the knowledge of who he was and how great his love was for me.

I thank God for his patience and loving kindness toward me in my state of brokenness. God's word is true; he said, "I have loved you, Felecia, with an everlasting love." When I was in the valley, he was with me because he said, "Lo, I am with you always, even until the end of time."

CHAPTER 2

Thanks for the Memories

MY FATHER DIED, suddenly, prior to my third birthday. Even though my time with my father was brief, God blessed me with vivid memories of our time together. I still remember the time he lovingly pushed me in a homemade swing made out of an old car tire and rope that was attached to a tree in the backyard of our four-family flat. Even now, when I close my eyes, I can feel the warmth of the sun's rays filtering through the leafy green branches of the tree nestled in our backyard. I can still hear the sounds of my laughter as I twirled in the directions the swing took me, and I can see Daddy's big smile and hearing his jolly laughter as he pushed me in that swing.

I remember the warm sunny day when Mom, Daddy, and I lounged on a blanket during a family picnic. I must have relished those moments together because I refused to get up when it was time to leave; I just lay there playing possum. Gingerly, Mom and Dad rolled me up like a cigar and carried me away—priceless!

I remember sitting at the breakfast table in the wee hours of the morning, watching Daddy eating his breakfast and preparing to go to work at Ford Motor Company. Sitting in my high chair, dazed and confused, looking out the window, where it was still dark outside, I was baffled, wondering why in the world we were sitting here eating breakfast! It was confusing to me because it was always sunny in the morning when we ate breakfast on the weekends.

I remember the time the family went on a helicopter ride, and I was eyeing my white high-tops and looking down on the cityscapes.

I remember the time Momma and Daddy were engaged in a heated verbal argument in the dining room of our upper flat. They were at opposite ends of the dining room table, yelling at each other as they circled the table. Every time Daddy made a move, Momma made a move. I had sided with Momma. I was trailing closely behind her, keeping my eyes on him. At one point, I guess Daddy wanted to drive his point home, shouting and pounding his fist on the dining room table. Momma followed suit, shouting and pounding her fist on the table. I settled the score by banging my tiny fist on the table and shouting something at Daddy in baby gibberish. At that very moment, Daddy stopped yelling and banging his fist and doubled over in laughter. Daddy could not stop laughing. To this very day, I love the sound of a man's genuine laughter.

My saddest memory of Daddy is the day I had to say goodbye to him. It was the day of his funeral. That day I had to say goodbye to the first man I ever loved and who loved me back unconditionally. The first man who made me laugh out loud. I had to bid farewell to the first man who took me by the hand and took me for long walks to Grandma's house.

According to Mom, Daddy had died of complications from pneumonia. Sadly, it was in the winter during the Christmas holidays. On the day of his funeral, family members had gathered together at Grandma's house. My two-and-half–year-old mind could not comprehend that Daddy had died and was to be buried on this particular day. Yet the peculiar behavior of the women in my family seemed even more incomprehensible to me.

The mood of the house was solemn. Each of the women, my older cousins and aunts, wore a black dress adorned with a strand of pearls. I love pearls to this day. There was a steady flow of traffic to the upstairs bathroom. Eventually, I found myself wandering up the stairs and standing in the doorway of the bathroom, and what I saw amazed me: my cousin in a black dress and high heels, unraveling wads of toilet paper and crying as she gathered the toilet paper from the roll. I just stood there motionless in the doorway. I don't even know if she felt my presence.

My next memory of that day was me seated beside Momma in the front of the funeral home, looking at Daddy for the last time. Momma was crying uncontrollably and dabbing her eyes with a tattered piece of tissue. I sat looking up at her, and I began crying too. I remember reaching up to her with all my might for a piece of her tattered tissue to dry my tears too. At two-and-a-half, I could not have possibly known how profound that day was, but something inside me did. I do not remember seeing Daddy lying in his coffin. I just remember how sad Momma was, and it made me sad.

After the funeral, I was seated in a car. I refused to budge and just sat there, stationary. A man, possibly a relative, asked me to move over a couple times. I did not move a muscle or bat an eye. He had to physically pick my little body up to move my body over into another seat in the car. Perhaps I was waging a strong protest, waiting for Daddy to come outside of that dreadful place and take me away on one of our great adventures. I lost someone very precious that day.

At the age of two and a half, I had lost a major attachment figure in my life, my daddy. At the time, I could not comprehend the finality of death. It was not until I became a clinical social worker that I learned the mental, physical, and emotional impact of his death and how it would affect my ability to bond and form close and healthy relationships. Clinically speaking, his death was the portal to the development of grief and loss, separation anxiety, and posttraumatic stress. When I was two and a half, these are the responses I may have possibly experienced:

- Sleep disturbances
- Changes in appetite
- Regressive behaviors
- Crying
- Tantrums
- Rebellion
- Aggressive behaviors
- Clinging behavior
- Separation anxiety
- Anger
- Yearning for the deceased

Losing Daddy at such a young age greatly affected my ability to bond and form healthy long-lasting relationships. I lost a significant figure in my developmental and formative years. A bond was broken. My protector was gone. My daddy, my hero, my teacher. He was supposed to keep the wolves at bay. Daddy was supposed to prepare me for life by teaching me life lessons. He was supposed to dry my tears and heal my hurts; that is how the story was supposed to end. Our story ended far too soon. I have spent a great part of my life trying to finish our story. I have always wondered how our story would have ended.

When I was with Daddy, I felt loved. I felt protected. I was Daddy's little girl. He loved to show me off during our outings. Then, the unthinkable happened; my hero, my foundation, my defender was gone. In a moment, in the twinkling of an eye, my life changed.

I can only imagine how many times I must have sat stoically waiting for him to walk through the front door or looked for him to meet me at the swing in the backyard or sit down for breakfast at the kitchen table or to take Mom and me to the park for a picnic. I can only imagine lying in bed waiting for him to tuck me in bed and kiss me good night. I can only imagine; it was not long before my excitement and anticipation finally waned and transformed into tears, sadness, grief, and finally anger. Perhaps that is why I found myself in a series of intimate relationships with male partners who were mentally and emotionally unavailable and detached. Unconsciously, I dated men who would abruptly walk out of my life without a moment's notice. Each time, I would find myself lingering by the telephone, checking my voice mail, or hoping to cross their paths. Soon my anticipation and excitement would turn to denial, anger, depression, and finally, over time, resignation. This cycle continued for years. I would be drawn to men who could not commit to a loving, long-term relationship. We would have a good time, and soon they were gone.

My father's death changed my mother's life and my baby sister's life as well as mine; eventually, it changed the dynamics of our living arrangements. After his death, we moved from our four-family flat and into in a basement unit of an apartment. I was in kindergarten when we moved into the apartment. One of my fondest memories of living in that apartment was the night my sister, Christine, and I were playing with our toys in our bedroom. Suddenly, we were interrupted by my mother's crying. Together we slowly walked into the living room and found Momma in a chair with her face buried in the palm of her hands, crying her eyes out. Christine and I climbed onto the chair and onto her lap, and we too began to cry. We laid our little heads on her bosom as we all cried together. I do not know what brought about Momma's tears, perhaps Daddy's death and the realization that she was a young widow alone raising two small children. I believe her tears were for everyone she had lost to death along the way. Mom had experienced her share of losses early on in her life. Her mother, Annie, died on Mom's third birthday. Her stepmother died when Mom was in her early twenties. After we all had a good cry, Momma made some cream of mushroom soup.

It was while we were living in that apartment that my gift for public speaking manifested itself. My mother was summoned to the school because the kindergarten teacher seemed to think I was a little chatterbox. The teacher assumed I must be an only child because of my vocal skills. Mom said that I listened to the teacher's prattling with my arms folded, impatiently tapping my Capezio shoes and sporting a look on my face that seemed to say, "What is her deal? This is me. I talk okay." Mom was tickled.

We lived in that basement unit until we had a break-in. We were attending a family outing when it happened. After the break-in, we moved. This move would prove to be life changing.

CHAPTER 3

Seasons of Change

1. *To EVERY thing there is a season, and a time to every purpose under the heaven*
2. *A time to be born, and a time to die; a time plant, and a time to pluck up that which is planted;*
3. *A time to kill, and a time to heal; a time to break down, and a time to build up;*
4. *A time to weep, and a time to laugh; a time to mourn, and a time to dance;*
5. *A time to cast away stones, and a time to gather stones together; a time to embrace, and a time to refrain from embracing;*
6. *A time to get and a time to lose, a time to keep and a time to cast away;*
7. *A time to rend, and a time to sew; a time to keep silence, and a time speak*
8. *A time to love, and a time to hate; a time of war, and a time of peace.*

—Ecclesiastes 3:1–8

~ Time Line~

Elementary School

I became a victim of sexual abuse and sexual exploitation, perpetrated by a classmate's teenage brother and his male teenage friend. I would visit her home to play with her dolls. I do not remember the particulars as to how and when it started, but the memories of the trauma have played out in my mind like a movie, taunting me for years. It was in her home where my childhood took a traumatic turn. Her brother and his friend would come into the room and have sex with me. I was still in elementary school. I must have been eight or nine years old. I can still remember the time he chased me around the room. I tried to run away; but he caught me, picked me up, and carried me to the couch. I started singing; I cannot remember the song. I was singing as loud as I could, but he still violated me sexually as he forced me down on the couch.

Then, there was the time he brought his male friend to the room. I remember him telling me, when he had finished, to go home and wash myself. After I got down off his lap, I obeyed. Those stinging words still resonate in my memory today. He spoke to me like a "dutiful father." I nodded my head and got up and left. How sick was that! A grown man violates me and covers his filthy deed. When I think about it now, I see what he did to me. He conditioned me to clean up his filth. He did not care about me; he only cared about himself. Sexual abuse is never ever about the victim. That is why it is called abuse. It is a violation. It is the infringement on the rights of others who are unable to fight back, advocate, or take a stance for themselves.

The sexual abuse would provide a blueprint for my relationships with men. I satisfied their needs and cleaned up myself. No ties, no attachments, no commitment. Just *wham; bam; thank you, ma'am*. The sexual abuse put me on a destructive path of relationships in which sex was primary. No conversation, commitment, or passion. Having sexual intercourse was the only way I could get them to hold me, touch me, and caress me. My mind-set was that I would take care of their physical needs and not my mental, physical, and emotional needs. I did nothing wrong. I was used. I was not damaged. I was violated.

I remember the time I witnessed a live sex act in my classmate's home. I was sitting in the family den with a host of friends from the neighborhood, male and female, all in their teens. I do not even know why I was in the den or why my friend was not present. These kids were close in age to my perpetrator. Suddenly, my offender began having sex with a teenage neighbor. Everyone just watched as the two of them did the deed in plain sight. There must have been at least ten people present, including the neighbor's younger brother. I sat in shock; I could not move! My eyes must have popped out of my head!

The trauma of being sexually abused changed me for the worse. In an instant, my childhood innocence was shattered. My virginity was stolen. My personal rights were trampled by a mentally ill person. A person has to be mentally ill to sexually abuse a child—something had to have gone terribly wrong in their life for them to commit such acts. Perhaps they too were a victim of sexual abuse. Sexual abuse is not about intimacy. It is about power and control. Do not mistake that power for strength because it is a weakness. You have to be weak to fondle and sexually abuse a helpless child. It's about terrorizing and intimidating a person who cannot physically defend herself. That is why the act and the abuser are shrouded in secrecy, often protected by parents, spouses, and family; nobody wants the rest of the family to know that there is a pervert in the camp because of a potential beat-down by sane family members. So they cover for the coward. This is a terrible, terrible mistake. The sexual abuser is sick and needs professional help.

The sexual abuse was my gateway to sexual promiscuity, alcohol, and substance abuse. I smoked marijuana for the first time at the age of twelve. My teenage neighbor and her boyfriend invited me over for a puff. I was not inhaling yet, but I was sure trying my best. By the time I was thirteen, I was smoking cigarettes and marijuana. I became sexually promiscuous. There was a time during my menstruation that I was "late." My mother was horrified. Thankfully, my period came, but that scare did not stop me. I continued to be promiscuous. To remedy the situation, my mother put me on birth control pills to prevent another such scare. My mother was working full time, raising two teenage daughters. She was not trying to become a grandmother. My mother wanted us to abstain at all cost, but she realized she could not be with us all the time.

My personal boundaries had been violated and trampled, my trust broken. The sexual abuse changed me. It opened the door to emotions and feelings I could not handle. One minute I was playing with cutout dolls and Barbie dolls, and the next minute, my underwear was being snatched off and I was being sexually molested. I could not process the feelings unleashed by sexual victimization. I was introduced to sensuality—there is the possibility that, as wrong as it was, it probably felt good. Suppressing those feelings manifested guilt, shame, and blame: I believed it was my fault the abuse happened.

For years I struggled with the concept that it felt good because it was not supposed to because I was a child being sexually assaulted. So the feelings of shame and guilt developed, and I felt dirty. As a young child, I took baths constantly. I guess that was my way of washing the filth of my offender off of me. During that time, my mom used a body and bath wash by Jean Naté. I loved the smell of it, but Mom told me to stop using it because it was for grown-ups. One time I washed myself in Jean Naté, believing Mom would not smell it; I was only eight or nine at the time, but Mom did indeed smell and whopped my behind good. Since that time, I have not used Jean Naté in my bath or shower. Even now, when I see it in the stores, I do not touch it. Sadly, I believe every time I see a bottle of Jean Naté in the drugstore, vivid memories of the sexual abuse and the physical discipline come back to me. As a work in progress, I eventually plan to purchase that lovely fragrance, splash it on, and celebrate my deliverance.

The fact that the sex may have felt good reinforces the shame factor. The shame barometer goes full tilt. It may have felt good, but I was at an age when I should *not* be enjoying *it*! I was a child forced to experience adult emotions and sensations that even some adults cannot process because they are caught up in the feeling of the moment. There was no way I could handle those feelings at such a young age. One Christmas holiday, the sensual side of me kicked in while I was sitting on my neighbor's lap in the backseat of a car as some family members were driving us to visit relatives. In those days, car seats and seat belts were not mandatory, so I was seated on my neighbor's lap. All of a sudden, I caught a "feeling"; I positioned myself on my neighbor's knee and began rocking back and forth. My neighbor yelled, "What are you doing!" I believe she whacked me on the side of my head. Startled, ashamed, and embarrassed, I immediately stopped. Needless to say, that never happened again.

As the sexual abuse progressed, I began to dress differently, more seductively, even though I was still in elementary school. What was going on inside began showing up on the outside. I would dress one way when I left the house, and then I would do a quick change once I got to school. In those days, we recycled clothing to the max. If a dress was too short, it was recycled and used as a large shirt, and you wore slacks underneath. Me, I would wear the short dress, tights, and slacks out of the house; but, once I got to school, I would remove my slacks and strut around the school in a mini dress. I got a lot of stares and disapproving glares from my classmates. I must have looked like a "hot" mess. For beginners, I was too heavy to wear that type of outfit. Secondly, it was totally inappropriate for a school setting or anywhere else for that matter.

Sadly, not one teacher or counselor pulled me to the side to inquire why I dressed that way. And, even if they had, it was the '60s, and counselors and teachers did not discuss "good touch and bad touch."

Internally, I knew what my offender was doing was wrong. Externally, I often felt really bad and dirty. I felt alone, and I wanted to cry out for help. I just did not know how to go about it. One day in school, I was walking the halls, and I wanted cry out for help, but I did not know where to go. I leaned against the wall wanting to scream, wanting to tell the "dirty little secret"—but to whom? The teachers didn't ask, or couldn't. And the other students didn't want anything to do with me, just as I didn't want anything to do with them. The more I isolated myself from them, the more they isolated themselves from me.

I began to implode and turn my anger inward. I gained weight and isolated myself. I found comfort in food and sweets. To mask my pain, I ate everything in sight! Suzy Q's was my food of choice. I let the boys in my class fondle me in ways you could not imagine because I thought that was what they were supposed to do. I would let them hump me as I sipped water from the water fountain. Afterward, I felt dirty and ashamed. I will never forget the time in class when I was wearing one of my short dresses, without tights this time, and I let a male classmate fondle my vagina under the table. A female classmate got suspicious and looked under the table. When she came up, she looked at me with total disdain. She just stared at me as if to say "you filth." I felt like dirt. She was a good friend at the time. That little escapade changed the nature of our relationship. It was not long before word spread throughout the school that I was an easy girl.

As the result of the sexual abuse, I was not a social butterfly in elementary school. I lacked self-esteem and confidence so I isolated myself from my classmates. Recreation was not my favorite school activity because of my classmates' refusal to pick me for their teams. I was the last picked for everything when it came to team-related activities. I remember cringing as I sat waiting in anticipation to be picked for the basketball team, baseball team, volleyball team, or four-square in the gymnasium while my classmates were being chosen. As the students were hand selected, they jumped up! I sat just there, head hung low, and, finally, when they got down to the final two, three, or four students left sitting, the team captains still struggled to make their selection. And then at last, my name was called. With my pride on the floor, I struggled to get up—feeling unwanted—and joined a team that did not want me. This happened all the time.

I was craving attention. I wanted to fit in with the crowd. During those days, basement parties were popular, and a classmate invited me to her party. Now, except for my sexual promiscuity, the boys in my class did not give me the time of day. However, when word got out that I was coming to the party, the boys in my class planned to gang rape me in the basement at the party. I learned about their scheme, but, because I had been sexualized, I was open to the possibility of a group of male classmates sexually assaulting me. The boys did not show up at the party, and I remember being highly upset. The sexual abuse had unleashed something horrible inside of me, dark and foreboding. The sensual feelings were very powerful. I was experiencing feelings and emotions too powerful for a young elementary-school girl. Thankfully, there was a light at the end of this emotional tunnel. In the midst of the turmoil, I found a healthy outlet to channel my feelings and emotions.

By the grace of God, I found comfort in reading books in elementary school. I read anything I could get my hands on. My first love, the stories of Dick and Jane and their dog Spot introduced me to the world of reading. I became a member of a book club sponsored by the school. Each month, students ordered books. Momma was very supportive of my desire to read and would let me purchase four or five books at a time. When the books were distributed, I would be the student with the most books. When my name was called to pick up my books, my chest would swell with pride as I walked to my desk with a stack of books. I even read some books twice if I ran out of books before it was time to order again. I remember one book in particular: *The Ghost of Windy Hill*. I loved that little spooky book. I read it twice! As time progressed, to save money, I would visit the public library and bookmobile to borrow books. Reading became an escape for me; books took me on adventures and to places I had never been, all from the comforts of my playroom at home.

In addition to reading, I enjoyed teaching. I had a chalkboard and a slew of books in my playroom. I had a table with chairs filled with teddy bears and dolls in class for their lessons. They got spanked if they got out of line. Spanking or paddling was allowed in school in the '60s.

Thankfully, I had a great mom who was an excellent money manager. After Daddy died, his social security and veteran's check generously provided for us. We did not go without. We always had shelter, food, and clothing. Mom did not mind riding public transportation. Mom would take my sister and me to the movies and plays in Downtown Detroit. Our fondest memories of Downtown Detroit were the Thanksgiving parade and Christmas on the twelfth floor of J. L. Hudson. It would be an annual family outing. Christine and I would shop for Christmas gifts at the "children's only" shop while Mom waited for us in the waiting area. Carnival rides and children's activities abounded on that floor. Later we would go to the Christmas carnival at Cobo Hall and have a blast sliding down the giant snowman. Mom made Christmas in that home spectacular. I will never forget the Christmas I got a color television set and three—count them—*three* Jackson 5 albums and an Elvis Presley album. Some of my best memories in that house were of watching Elvis Presley on television or listening to his records because that was my "me time," when no one—and I mean *no one*—could disturb me. One time I was listening to "Kentucky Rain" by Elvis Presley when my cousin came into my bedroom and snatched the record off the turntable. I screamed in horror; my aunt, his mother, had worked the late shift the night before and was aroused from her sleep by my cries. She stomped into my bedroom, assessed the scene, and beat the crap out of him!

On weekends, we would visit the Detroit Institute of Arts and the Detroit Historical Museum. I fell in love with the Detroit Historical Museum at a young age. When I was old enough, Christine and I would catch the bus and just hang out there for hours. To this day, it is still my favorite place! Once a month, we would have a great steak dinner at the Flaming Embers in Downtown Detroit. Talk about good eating! Steak, potatoes, salad, a beverage, and dessert—and we consumed it all in one setting. No doggie bags: just scraps.

We loved shopping in Downtown Detroit. We bought our school clothes from Crowley's and J. L. Hudson's. Hudson's had a children's shoe department that housed a castle. You would try your shoes on and strut to the castle to see if they fit okay. We would have hot dogs and hot waffles and ice cream sandwiches in Kresge's Department Store after buying cutout dolls upstairs. One of Christine's fondest memories was of munching on a hot dog while looking out of Kresge's huge window at the Christmas lights and Santa's Castle adorning J. L. Hudson's across the street.

The sexual abuse was taking an emotional toll. I was imploding because I was keeping everything inside. There is a saying: sexual-abuse victims are "secret keepers." Some secrets are never meant to be kept. However, I harbored this secret for years. Who was I going tell? How was I going to tell? I was scared.

One day, I had reached a boiling point in the classroom. I had got into a shoving match with a female classmate. We were passing licks back and forth when, suddenly, she hit me in the eye. From that point on, everything went black. I mean really black. A fistfight broke out between us. I do not remember any details of the fistfight. My classmates had to give me the play-by-play action when I came to my senses. After the fight, my eyes opened to a classroom in shambles. Desks were knocked over on their sides, books and papers littered the floor. The coat closet was in disarray, and my only question was, "Who won?!" I do not remember the fight. I just remember a teacher yanking on me hard as she pulled me up from the floor. Without question, my mother was summoned to the school to meet with school officials, and I was referred to a mental-health professional, which was to be the first of many visits.

My next-door neighbor was a party animal; there were always parties at her house. One night, I was playing the "little barmaid," making sure everybody had ice and chasers for their drinks. My neighbor had a brother, a grown man, who was short in stature and a lot of fun to hang around with. He would play with the kids on the block. On this particular night, the party was in full swing. I was sent to the kitchen to get ice. I had the freezer door open, and her brother came into the kitchen grabbed me and tried to kiss me! I was about twelve years old! He got me in a tight embrace; I didn't scream because I didn't want to get him in trouble, but we were struggling hard, and—that close up—I could see his missing teeth as he puckered his lips to kiss me. Finally, he loosed his grip and let me go. I did not say a word to anyone. I was in shock.

Several days later, he was staying at his sister's house next door because his sister and her family were set to go out of town. I was standing on my front porch waving goodbye to the family when, all of a sudden, I heard glass breaking, followed by a blood-curdling scream, and I saw his bloodied face slam through the front window. Blood and glass were everywhere. The family slowly turned back and returned to the house. Later, I learned that, as he walked to the window to bid the family a safe trip, he lost his balance and crashed through the front window. He survived, but I kept my distance from him.

One of my saddest memories on record is of an incident that occurred one summer in the '70s. I was a preteen, wearing a multi-colored, polyester mini-dress, stockings, and black patent-leather boots—in the summertime. I was sitting on my next-door neighbor's front porch, listening to the soulful sounds of Al Green. My neighbor loved to party, and she loved, loved, *loved* Al Green. She would fry up some chicken, fish, cornbread, and butter beans, put out some Ripple and Annie Green Spring wines, and host a spontaneous get-together for her friends, family, and people from the neighborhood. The place was rocking and was packed with men and women.

As I sat on the front porch, my mother's boyfriend came by unexpectedly. I could tell that he was not in a good mood. He looked at the house in anger and agitation. He did not enter the house but told me to go get my mother. I jumped up and went into the house and told my mother that her boyfriend was outside waiting for her. I neglected to mention that he looked angry, too. Once she came out on the porch, he wanted her to go next door to our house I tagged along because I was having trouble with the zipper on my boot.

Once inside the house, I flopped down on the sofa while my mother and her boyfriend stayed in the hallway near the living room. I was tugging on my boot zipper when I heard screams coming from the hallway. I sprang into action, running in the direction of the screams, and found my mother's boyfriend beating her, punching her in the stomach with his fist, beating her badly. I began to scream and cry while attempting to pound him on his back with my fist, but he kept beating her. I knew I had to get help.

So I bolted and ran out the front door and down the walkway and over to my neighbor's house. I could have just cut across the front yard, but I was hysterical. I ran up my neighbor's walkway; I saw her teenage daughter sitting in a chair on the front porch with several men. I fell in her lap, sobbing hysterically. I could not breathe. I could not catch my breath. It was as if the air had been sucked out of my lungs. The men on the front porch sat motionless. Finally, after what seemed liked forever, I mouthed the words, pointing my finger toward the house next door, "He hit her!"

What happened next still amazes me; the men on the banister jumped off the banister, never taking the stairs and headed to the house. The partygoers inside the house got wind of the fight next door and emptied out the house and bolted next door. Everybody was next door.

When he came out of that house, he was a bloody mess. His shirt was torn. He was staggering. He scrambled to get away in his car. By this time, word spread throughout the neighborhood, and neighbors came running to aid and assist a sister in peril. Someone threw a cinder block and blocked the wheel of his car. He was trapped again. They busted out his car windows, headlights, and taillights, and yanked him out of the car and continued kicking his behind. I saw someone was in the kitchen boiling hot water and lye to douse him. Oh, yes, it was on and popping!

When I think back now, I believe the men who were sitting on the porch sensed something bad was going to happen because, when Momma's boyfriend came to the house initially, I was sitting alone on the front porch. It was after we left to go home next door that the men sat outside. No one liked her boyfriend because of his jealousy and anger. Thank God for those men and everyone in the house and on the block who helped her that day. I do not want to imagine how things could have turned out had they not been looking out for her safety.

After the fireworks, my mother sat my sister and me down and said we would never see him again. I went to bed feeling safe. All was right with the world until he showed up one day and announced they were a couple again. I was filled with shock, confusion, anger, and resentment. I hated him. I hated him for years. The abuse continued, and they continued to get back together, and I was punished for hating him. He brought nothing but division and conflict to the family. It would culminate later in life in a way that surprised the entire family.

My sister and I were in our early twenties, at home with Mom when her abusive boyfriend brought her some fresh catfish. Now, she had never cleaned any type of fish in her life. He dropped them off and left the house despite her telling him that she did not want the fish.

The catfish, with huge nasty whiskers, were swimming around in a bucket of water. Not thinking he would return, she gave the bucket of nasty fish to a neighbor who could cook, clean, chop, and skin anything that moved.

Suddenly, the boyfriend came back, demanding his catfish. She informed him that she had given them away to a neighbor. He got mad, real mad. His voice was rising, and her voice was shaking.

They were in the dining room. She was sitting, and he was standing, interrogating her. Her head was hung low, and her voice was just above a whisper. He wanted his fish or his money. She did not have either. My sister was in the living room. We had a collie; sensing danger toward his master he began to bark. I was in the kitchen washing a big silver butcher knife. I knew what I had to do. I was not feeling good about it, but I was not going let this man beat my mother again. The beating I witnessed as a child played over and over in mind during the course of my life.

I began walking toward the dining room with butcher knife clutched in my hand when, all of a sudden, Christine jumped up and began cussing him out. I mean she emptied the chamber with a barrage of cusswords. She was already in the dining room telling him to get out. I froze with the butcher knife in hand. He stopped cussing and looked around in amazement; I guess he figured, unlike the beating I witnessed as a child, that this beat-down was going to have a little twist. He left the house. I mean he left without uttering a word. He never came back. Christine, the dog, and I had settled it once and for all.

Thank God for his divine presence. My life could have been dramatically altered if I had carried out that carving-knife defense.

Middle School

As my life spiraled out of control, I made several suicide attempts, believing that death would bring about peace.

At age thirteen, I attempted suicide for the first time. I do not recall all the factors that led to the action to end my life. I am sure that my father's death and the trauma of being sexually and physically abused were key factors. I attempted to take my life by taking a handful of orange pills. I must have swallowed at least twenty or more pills. My mom and sister were away at the time. A friend came to visit, and she and I sat on my front porch, lost in our own thoughts; as we watched the sunset. My friend was not much into conversation. She was perfect for that day because I did not want to discuss what I was about do: take my life. Sitting quietly in my lounge chair, I took special interest in the radiant sunset that evening because I believed was it going to be my last. I thank God for the blood of Jesus because that night, I threw up all night long. I kept throwing up the orange casings of the capsules I swallowed. No one knew I had ingested those pills.

My mother worked days at the time, and she woke me early that morning to lock the front door behind her; and that is when I collapsed. *Bam!* My body hit, slammed against the door, and I slid down. I only remember darkness, and, suddenly, I was awakened by my mother pounding on the front door. She had heard my body bang against the door. That was when she became suspicious. She knew I was on something. She scolded me and told how a young girl on a television show had taken her own life using pills. I too had heard the story. I grew up watching that show. I never told my mother I had tried to take my life.

My mother required major surgery, which would cause her to be hospitalized for several days. At the time, we lived in a two-family flat. Christine and I stayed alone, upstairs, during my mother's hospital stay. One of my aunts and her family lived directly across the street. Our neighbor downstairs lived with her two children. I do not know what came over me, but, one night, I put on a hat and dark sunglasses and set out to a liquor store. I was thirteen. The first time I bought a pint of hard liquor, I had no trouble buying it. I came home and drank my liquor. The next time I went to the store in my disguise, the clerk said, "This is the last time I will sell you liquor with those glasses and hat on." And she sold me the pint. This time, the liquor had a different effect. I tripped out and scared the crap out of my little sister, Christine. She called the neighbor downstairs, who came upstairs to check on me, but Christine said she was of no help at all. The lady hated me and was making fun of me. Poor Christine called my mother, who had just had surgery, and told her about my dilemma. Mom placed a call to her older sister, who lived about fifteen minutes away, to check on my drunk self. My poor aunt woke up her young grandchildren and caught a taxicab to come check on me. Needless to say, when my aunt arrived, my neighbor slithered back downstairs. My aunt stayed with us the rest of the evening.

On a good note, it was in middle school that I developed my love for cooking. I joined a home-economics club and had a ball. I learned to cook and sew. I was so engrossed in cooking that my teacher selected me to help facilitate cooking classes. One time, I cooked with a group of male students. They were so attentive and engaged in the cooking process. They wanted everything to be just right. It is still amusing to think of that day when our vegetable dish was peas with pearl onions. I can say that it was a wonderful experience. The guys were excellent students under my instruction. I still enjoy cooking and baking today.

High School

I was struggling academically as a student in high school. I would skip class, smoke weed in the girl's bathroom, and refuse to do my homework. I would spend my days walking the hall and eluding the hall monitors. Back then, report cards were handwritten, so grades could easily be altered. An E could be changed into a B. An F grade was definitely made into a B grade. Then you would get a buddy to forge the teacher's signature, and viola! You had passing marks and dodged a lifelong punishment of no television, no telephone, and a good butt whooping. For the most part, I did my schoolwork and got good grades when I was not getting high.

I sold weed in the neighborhood and school for the mother of one of my sister's friends. This lady, who knew my mother, asked me to sell it for her. In return, I was allowed to smoke weed in her house with her kids in the next room. She would roll big fat joints for me to sell, and they sold like hot cakes! One of my cousins tried to get me to skim the profits by splitting the joints in half because they were so big. Nope, not me. I was a drug seller with a conscience and with ethics. I did not want to short my boss. I was a big joke among my peers. My mother's boyfriend had gotten wind of my weed-smoking escapades and warned me that I would go on to something stronger one day if I continued smoking weed. I took a firm stance and said I would not!

One of my female friends was dating a guy who sold drugs—weed and pills, like Strawberry THC. I had never indulged in pill-taking, but my friend did. She put me up to asking her boyfriend to sell me a "hit" of a pill of Strawberry THC. I said, "Okay." That night we met him in front of her house, which were a few houses away from my house. A streetlight was shining brightly on his face as he stood in front of me with my friend at his side. So I asked him for a hit of Strawberry THC. What happened next had forever changed my life.

His nostrils flared; his eyes grew dim, then looked like they lit up red; his lips curled, and in a raised voice and filled with expletives, he said, "Don't you *ever* ask me for a blanking 'hit' of this *bleep*——— again. I should kick your *bleep*——— and tell your mother. Get your *bleep*———! back home!" I was startled and shaken, looking at my friend to throw me a line. She had put me up to asking in the first place. But she said nothing. She would not even look at me. I walked away with my tail tucked between my legs and N-E-V-E-R asked for a pill from him or anyone else E-V-E-R. He may have saved my life that night.

Prior to graduating from high school, I was a victim of rape perpetrated by the manager of a fast-food restaurant where I worked, a restaurant that's still in operation today. Like any teenager, I wanted to earn extra money to buy things, and this was my first job. My manager scared me; he would bark orders and embarrass me in front of customers when the lobby was filled with customers. Because he scared me, I used to stare, wide-eyed at him. He misinterpreted those looks I gave him, taking them as a sign that I was fascinated by him. I was by no means attracted to him. As a matter of fact, I found him repulsive.

He crossed the line and did the unthinkable one day. I was in the basement of the restaurant preparing for my workday. He was in the office talking on the telephone. He waved for me to come into the office. I was hesitant at first because I thought I was in trouble. I had on my uniform and my hat. We wore hats back then. He continued his phone conversation, but he never took his eyes off me. I started getting nervous. Suddenly, he ended his call. I was standing with my back against the wall. I will never forget—it was a wood-paneled wall. To this day, I do not like wood paneling. He pushed me against the wall, yanked my uniform pants and underwear down, unfastened his pants, and entered me right there in the basement of a busy restaurant. Unable to move, I stood like a corpse. I could not believe what was happening. It was as if I were in a bad dream. When he was done, he told me to fix myself and go back to work. I did just that. I went back upstairs to my workstation. I guess you could say I was in shock or just numb. I did not tell a soul for several days.

I will never forget the night I finally said something to somebody. My baby sister, Christine, and my cousin and I were sitting on the front porch of my home. It was night time. I remember the streetlight illuminating the porch. We were all sitting and talking when I abruptly said, "[——] raped me at work the other day." All of a sudden, my sister began to cry. I mean really cry. Her face was glistening with tears as the streetlight shined on her face. She was crouched over and wailing. She would not stop crying. As she cried, she could not take her eyes of me. To this day, I still cannot describe the hurt and pain I saw in her eyes. She was bawling like a baby. I stood in amazement, more puzzled than anything else.

Do not get me wrong. I was violated. I was hurt, but the effects of the trauma had numbed me. This was the first reaction I had ever received from anyone since the sexual victimization had begun, 'way back in my childhood. Never had I told anyone anything. I had kept it all inside. My feelings and emotions had shut down. I was like the walking dead. Christine's tearful reaction started a chain reaction because my cousin started crying too. I still cannot remember if I cried. Christine said, "We have to tell Momma!" *Tell Momma?* I was thinking to myself. Then, I knew it was serious. My mother was asleep, so we climbed the stairs to our upstairs flat and woke her up tell her the news. Momma was devastated. Family members were alerted. I was consoled.

Law enforcement was notified. I was questioned by police, but I was afraid to face my offender in court. Filled with shame, blame, and guilt, I stayed home from school for several days. I did not get counseling after the rape, so I continued to medicate myself by smoking weed and drinking. I felt comforted in the haze of weed and alcohol because I was not hurting when I was high. I blamed myself for what happened. I blamed myself for not telling my mother sooner.

I had continued to work under the authority of the rapist, and he continued to humiliate me in front of customers, but he never touched me again. I felt I had done something to deserve it. I thought maybe, if I had not stared at that ugly man, it might have never happened. My mother was baffled. She had visited the restaurant on several occasions to check on me. She had seen the manager on many occasions. He knew her. She may have even visited the restaurant the day the rape happened. After the rape was reported, I quit my job.

At the age of seventeen or eighteen, I would babysit my younger cousin who was around nine or ten years old. Sitting in the house babysitting a kid was not my thing. I was doing it for the money and as an outlet to smoke cigarettes and weed away from home. To spice things up, a couple of times I took her to a neighborhood bar to sit, drink, and listen to the music.

She would have a soft drink while I drank the hard stuff. No one, not one barmaid, bartender, or manager asked for my ID. Because of these little escapades at the neighborhood bar, my little cousin always wanted me to babysit her. We became hanging buddies. My cousin never told her mom until we were much older. As a matter of fact, this kid hung out with me during my early Marygrove days. She stayed at the dorm and even attended a Halloween party with me.

Marygrove College

After graduating from Central High School in Detroit, Michigan, I entered Marygrove College in Detroit, Michigan, in the fall of 1979. I will never forget that sunny September day when my mother drove through the wrought iron gates leading to the massive driveway of the college. I was in awe as I observed the beautiful gothic buildings and beautifully manicured lawns of the campus. As I, with a big wide grin, took in the splendor of the campus, Mom said, with a big, wide grin, "Felecia! Your life is going to change forever." If only I had held on to her encouraging words! If only I had believed her and believed in myself.

It was not until I got into in the twelfth grade that the subject of college came up between Mom and me. Mom was asking me what I was going to do with my life. For me, college had no value because I did not personally know of anyone who had been to college. Prior to attending Marygrove College, I had never even visited a college campus. My family members were factory workers. They were laborers at Ford, Chrysler, and General Motors. They worked hard Monday through Friday. Went to clubs and played Bingo in Canada on the weekends, played the lottery, paid the bills, brought groceries, and started the same routine Monday morning, back to the assembly line. That was life as I knew it.

As a rambunctious eighteen year old, I had plans to move to New York and live with my aunt in Harlem and work at Macy's Department Store as she did for many years. I was revving to go. When I told my mother my future plans, Mom said, "Absolutely not!"

What?! I had always had dreams of living in New York. The glamour, shopping, excitement, and parties—and Mom said *no*?

So I re-strategized and promptly informed her that I was going to join the armed forces. Which branch of the armed services I cannot begin to tell you because I said it in anger. Which would have been a dumb move seeing that I would not have made it through basic training, being the "neat freak" that I am. I saw a basic-training drill while visiting Camp Pendleton in San Diego, California, in 1985. My friend's husband, who was a Marine, had taken me on a tour of the base. I watched as a soldier did a drill and missed a step and slammed into a pool mud and water. I promptly asked my friend's husband if he was going to take a shower, and he said, "No, he has to keep going in the soaked, muddied uniform." I stared with horror as the soldier continued the drill in dirty, muddy clothes.

Momma did not utter a word to me when I broke the news about joining the armed services. But, several days later, I got a visit from her big brother, my Uncle Benny (or Big Ben), who politely got in my face and went on a rant of verbal expletives, saying, "If you ever make your mother cry again about some *bleep*—— of you joining the *blanking* army, I will kick yo' *bleep*—— myself, you hear me?" *Yes, sir!* Needless to say, the armed-services discussion never came up in our home again I promptly took my SATS/ACTS and brought my high-school grade-point average up to a 2.5. I eventually made the honor roll before graduation. Mom completed my financial-aid application; we attended college orientation, and I enrolled into Marygrove College—all the while looking over my shoulder for Uncle Benny.

Marygrove College held students to a standard of academic excellence and still does. As a student, I fell short. I did well academically in some courses and failed miserably in others. My poor academic habits from high school had carried over to college. I just would not study and apply what I had been taught. Math presented the biggest problem because I hadn't mastered basic mathematics in high school. I believe I failed algebra three times in high school because I had never mastered basic math: addition, subtraction, division, and multiplication which are foundations for mathematical success. It was pitiful.

I was not academically challenged; I was just L-A-Z-Y. My philosophy was that I was never going apply math to anything in my life so why bother? That juvenile philosophy came back and bit me in the behind a hundred times over. I quickly learned math and science applied to everything in life, forever! Just ask my checking account. Try figuring the 20-percent discount on a $39.99 item. It's going to involve math. Trying figuring how a pilot and air-traffic controller can navigate a flight to Florida. Or how square footage and prices for flooring come together. Math! Marygrove College offered resources such as tutoring to assist me, but my P-R-I-D-E resulted in me declining help. I did not want the student body to know I was struggling academically. As if I was the only one experiencing academic difficulties. Many students were, and that is why the school offered those resources. Asking for help is not a sign of weakness. It is a major strength, in every area of your life, to acknowledge shortcomings and seek assistance. Nobody knows everything all the time, with the exception of God.

When I was nineteen, my second suicide attempt garnered me a stay in a psychiatric hospital. I was on the verge of being dismissed from Marygrove College for poor academic performance. I went to my dorm room and took a handful of pills. I got scared, so I called a friend and told her what I had done, and she came to my aid and rushed me to a hospital emergency room. After being evaluated, I was admitted to a psychiatric hospital. I later learned that, when my mother and sister heard what had happened, they cried all night long.

With the exception of the 6:00 a.m. blood draws, the first few days at the hospital were actually relaxing. Nobody bothered me, and I did not bother them. Then, one morning, the funniest thing happened. A group of us were lined up on our way to an art class when a patient broke rank and started walking in another direction. The staff asked the patient where was he going, and he answered, bewildered, "To get my shampoo." I started laughing and I could not stop. I said to myself, *These people are crazy!* After a few days, I met with the psychiatrist and posed a question, "Doctor, am I copping out?" The psychiatrist started laughing out loud. I mean really cracking up without ever answering my question. So I figured he had answered my question. My mother had come to the hospital for a visit to drop off clean clothes for me. I told her to wait because I was signing myself out, and I hightailed it out of there.

My mother worked with me academically by getting me tutors in math, but I would not apply what I learned. In essence, I just gave up. I did not want to conform to the academic culture of college discipline and commitment. *Why?* you ask. Because I wanted to hang on to my weed-smoking buddies and a lifestyle of partying all night long while going to college.

After receiving several written and verbal warnings from the college's academic-review board, I was dismissed from Marygrove College in the winter of 1982—during the Christmas holiday to be exact.

At our home, the house was decorated. The Christmas tree was beautiful, and all was right with the world. What sat in the mailbox brought my world to a crashing halt. I immediately recognized the envelope containing my grades. What surprised me was the letter from Marygrove included along with those grades. I had never gotten this type of letter before. I knew what was concealed in that letter was not going to be good.

I opened the sealed envelope; it contained my letter of dismissal from the college. I had been dropped from the college. Suddenly, things were not festive and merry anymore. I read the letter silently and then again, aloud, through my tears and with a raspy voice, to my mother, who was sitting on the living-room couch. I remember so vividly my mom sitting on that couch as I read the letter. Mom was heartbroken. She sat in silence, but her facial expression said it all. Her hopes and dreams that I would be the first in the Berry family to earn a college education were gone. Boy, did I cry! I cried like a baby because deep down I knew I had thrown away a wonderful opportunity at an outstanding college all for a lifestyle of drugs, sex, and alcohol.

My dismissal should not have come as a surprise. Everybody was working with me, trying to keep me there: the counselor, the nurse, the nuns, the tutors, and my classmates. I had been warned repeatedly by my academic advisor. The college offered resources such as counseling and tutoring. Students would invite me to study with them, but I chose not to study. I did not see the value in obtaining a college education. No one in my family had ever received a college education. None of my weed-smoking high-school buddies were in college, nor were they talking about the possibility of going.

Wayne County Community College

To save face, I enrolled in Wayne County Community College (downtown campus) to take the classes I failed at Marygrove College. I took algebra, humanities, English, psychology, art history, and typing. I fell in love with art history. I absolutely love art. I was so good in art history that the instructor asked me to teach a class one day. I was an outstanding student. I got A's and B's. I excelled in math. I left prior to completing my associate's degree.

On the downside, I was living a lie. I was going to Wayne County Community College every day while staying in the dorm at Marygrove

College, pretending to be a student at Marygrove. Get it? I was ashamed that I was dismissed from the college, so I lived a lie, told everybody the lie until I could not afford the dorm anymore. To be truthful, many of the students were becoming suspicious because they never saw me in any classes. *Duh.*

The decision to attend Wayne County Community College would later prove to be a wise move. While attending the community college, I met some wonderful classmates and had many wonderful experiences.

CHAPTER 4

The Valley

Yea, though I walk through the valley of the shadow of death, I will fear
no evil; for thou art with me; thy rod and thy staff, they comfort me.

—Psalms 23:4

Yes, though I walk through the [deep, sunless] valley of the shadow
of death, I will fear or dread no evil, for You are with me; Your
rod [to protect] and Your staff [to guide], they comfort me.

—Psalms 23:4 (Amplified Bible)

AFTER MY DISMISSAL from Marygrove College, my life changed
dramatically. I had hit bottom. I got on general assistance or welfare because
I was unable to find employment. I received a biweekly stipend and food
stamps. I worked in housekeeping at International Business Machines (IBM).
Yep, I cleaned toilets, mopped floors, and emptied trash containers.

I drank alcohol to compensate for the succession of bad choices that
I had made in my personal life. Laden with the shame, blame, and guilt
of harboring the secret of my early childhood sexual victimization and
the trauma of being raped as a teen, I systematically fostered a poor
opinion of myself. Mentally, I labeled myself as damaged goods and acted
accordingly.

My life was just a big puff of weed smoke. I was living for the moment and not for a lifetime. I became a party girl. I partied in the clubs, parks, and basements. One year for my birthday, I partied all night long. When I came outside, the sun was rising, and I still had a drink in my hand. On another night, I went to a club, and no one asked me to dance, so I took matters into my own hands. When the DJ played my favorite song, and with liquor in my system, I marched to the stage—not the dance floor—and danced. One of my female cousins joined me! My sister and my other female cousin looked up from the dance floor in horror! Everybody else just joined in.

I did another crazy dance during the boat races at the Belle Isle Park in Detroit, Michigan. My cousin and her husband would camp out the night before. I had joined them. After a few drinks, I began to dance, and her husband began to film me. While dancing provocatively, I simulated removing my clothes. For years, he has taunted me with that film footage; now the secret is out. However, I have changed my dance habits. I dance before the Lord now, and I give it all I got, just like David when he danced. I have been told by fellow parishioners that I have been on camera during praise and worship dancing before the Lord in front of the whole congregation!

In my early twenties, I was at a point in my life where I did not care what the future held because, as a trauma survivor, death was always at the forefront of my mind. I never made plans because a little voice inside my head always told me I was going to die. The thought of death came out of nowhere.

The first time the thought hit me was one sunny afternoon in Greektown—an area of Downtown Detroit, a festive city block in the heart of the city, which sells everything Greek. Greek food, salads, flaming cheese, olives, shish kebabs, desserts—you name it. Christine, my sister, and I had a wonderful lunch and decided to do a little retail therapy. We found a wonderful clothing store that had awesome shoes, clothes, and purses. The bonus was that the store offered layaway. I found the pair of shoes of my dreams and was planning to put them in layaway when suddenly a voice said, "Don't put them in the layaway 'cause you are going to die." Shaken, I put the shoes down, and a feeling of despair came over me. I was scared, but I did not say anything to Christine. I did not know what to say. I did not want to scare her.

That day marked an important point in my cycle of unfinished plans, goals, and dreams. The thought of death, my death, hindered my purpose and potential for a great part of my life. Everything was placed on hold because I thought I was going to die. So I lived recklessly. I threw all caution to the wind. What I would later learn was that voice I heard was from the devil, Satan, my enemy. I believed his lie and acted upon it because I did not know or have a relationship with God or God's truth.

I would find myself in compromising situations because of the alcohol and substance abuse. Drinking clouded my judgment. I was a major risk taker. I was not afraid of the dark. I would go to liquor stores as late as 11:00 p.m. I hated to run out of liquor. One night, I was in a liquor store, and it was late. All of a sudden, I heard a voice say, "Look around; you are the only woman in the store." I froze and looked around the store, and all the customers were men. God had sent me a warning, and I high-tailed it out of there. That night, I was delivered from late-night liquor-store runs.

To make some quick money, I tried to get into the illegal numbers game. I would take down numbers via telephone and, for a fee, play them for people. In other words, I stood in the long lottery lines and played the numbers for my clients. If they hit the lottery, they would sometimes give me a tip.

I went to drug houses to buy drugs to get high. Sometimes babies in diapers would bring the bag of weed to the door. Sometimes the dealers would be perfect strangers to me and my friends. We would meet these drug dealers on the street or at a club, and they would say, "Hey, come on over to my house!" And we would go!

There were times when I engaged in illicit sex acts with strangers whom I met after a night of partying. One night, after leaving a male dance show, I was walking to my car, and a man whom I had never seen before was standing near my car. As I was about to get into my automobile, he greeted me, and I responded. He seemed nice; what could be wrong with a guy dressed in a suit and tie at 2:00 am? *Duh!* That was the alcohol thinking for me. Well, one thing led to another, and I found myself in the basement of this stranger's home having sex in total darkness. At one point, in the dark, he reached for something. I do not know what it was. So I reached for his hand, and he jumped. I thought he was going to pull a weapon. I was so scared. By God's grace, I got dressed and got out of there.

Once, I went to a motorcycle club with a friend of mine. Motorcycle clubs were not my normal mode of partying because they scared me to death. The bikers' idea of partying was a little different than what I was used to. For starters, I did not like their security system, which consisted of barring the door by putting a slack of wood across the entrance. Women were dancing naked with five to ten guys crowded around them. Drugs like cocaine were used in the open.

My friend and I had separated. I was looking for the restroom in the darkness of the club, and a man in jeans, cowboy boots, and a cowboy hat asked if he could be of assistance. Silly me said, "Yes, I am looking for the women's restroom." He led me to a door that blended into the wall and opened it, revealing the restroom, and he tried to enter in with me. Honestly, I believe the urine dried up inside me! I do not even remember using the toilet. I made haste to find my friend. It seemed as if the room had gotten bigger, the music had gotten louder, and the number of people had increased, and I could not find my friend. The room was dark. The walls were dark. Everything was dark! Finally, I thought, *I will leave her and drive home myself*—and there she was, sitting on a couch, watching me the whole time—grinning. She found my distress comical. That was the last night I hung with her or went to a motorcycle club.

Finally, I enrolled in a job-training program that landed me a position at a bank in Downtown Detroit. I started on midnights and was eventually promoted to the day shift, working on the main switchboard.

I worked at that bank switchboard for close to ten years, and suffered a lot in the process. It was a very busy switchboard, so the work was demanding, but—more than that—it was an awful work environment: I had one coworker who used the entire eight-hour day to bully and intimidate me. And my other coworkers weren't much better. They were four middle-aged women, and I was in my early twenties at the time. Each of them had her own story to tell—about divorce, a troubled marriage, problems with their children. Me, I was young, single, and childless, which prompted resentment on my coworkers' part. My problems were not their problems.

One coworker, like my cousin, said her life was over. She had started out in college and never finished, and she said her life was over and that she was destined to work the switchboard until retirement. I sat there listening but not agreeing. While working at the bank, I often thought about going back to Marygrove College and obtaining my degree. I had to believe that I would not retire from the bank working the switchboard.

The desire of my heart was to have a marketable skill that would open wide the doors of opportunity in an employment sector of my liking. I wanted to move from taking whatever employment I could get to getting the job that I wanted. Without a marketable skill or trade, I was only qualified for entry-level positions, often low paying. I began to write down the amount of money I wanted to make. Because I wanted to be a professional, I began to dress professionally. My sister had given me a red Coach briefcase as encouragement, and I began to walk the grounds of the municipal buildings in Downtown Detroit, imagining that I was a professional working the job of my dreams.

The transformation from wanting to be a professional to actually becoming one did not occur overnight. I learned that I had an outstanding debt with Marygrove College. I made arrangements and, over time, paid the bill in full. My job as a switchboard operator was emotionally grueling. At one point, in sheer desperation, I wrote the Marygrove College academic-review board a letter to request readmission into Marygrove College. I was at my wit's end working the busy switchboard at the bank, and I wanted out so badly that I took a spiral notebook and handwrote a letter pleading with Marygrove College to let me back in! I am 100-percent certain I did not proofread it. Needless to say, I received my denial letter, typed. I am so thankful; I serve a God not of a second chance but a God of another chance!

Yes, I made bad choices—skipping class and neither studying nor applying myself—and forfeited my opportunity to go to college. As a result, I was now suffering the consequences: an unsatisfying, low-paying job. During the downtimes, I would sit at my desk and write down my dreams, hopes, and desires for the job I wanted to have. I then put my faith in motion; I carried my briefcase to work. I rode the shuttle bus; it cost a little more, but I was riding with the professionals. I got flack from my coworkers about that, but I kept riding because I was on a mission. During my lunch hour, I used to walk through the City County Building, which is now the Coleman A. Young Municipal Building, envisioning that I was there on business. I would walk to Thirty-sixth District Court and stand outside and envision myself going in to do business. I was dreaming *big*! I was applying my faith in the midst of what I was going through on the job. I would read the classified section of the *Michigan Chronicle* at my desk every week. Each week there would be a plethora of classified ads for social workers.

Family members and friends had arrived and applied their God-given talents before me, utilizing those talents to realize their dreams. The door was still open to me too—wide open; I just had to walk through. The sky was the limit. I acknowledged the Lord, and he led me to and directed me on the path I needed to follow. The truth of the matter is, many people do not want to go through the process—in other words, do the work, make the sacrifice, and put in the time, effort, and hours. They just want it handed to them on a silver platter. Where is the glory in that? Faith without works is *dead*! If you have ever been thirsty, you can get a nice refreshing drink from the faucet, but you have to turn it on, and the water will flow, and you can have as much as you want for as long as you want—but you have to have to turn the water on.

In May of 1986, tragedy struck. I was sitting in the comfort of my living room, reading the metro section of a Detroit newspaper. The metro section listed the happenings, good and bad, that occurred in Oakland, Macomb, and Wayne counties. While I was skimming the local stories, one particular news item caught my attention. A murder had occurred in the city. The article said that a disgruntled man had shot and killed his former wife. I was stunned; I sat thinking to myself, *How sad for that poor lady to have met such a bad fate.* I proceeded to read the next story.

About a half an hour later, my telephone rang; it was a cousin calling to inform me that our cousin had been shot and killed by her former husband. He said the story was in the newspaper. I froze. I could not form words to come out of my mouth. It was my cousin's death story in the metro section of the newspaper? My thoughts were racing. I was thinking, *This happens to other people—not to us! This was my cousin! This is my family!* This was my cousin whom I used to see frequently at Grandma's house. The cousin whose wedding I attended as a little girl on Dexter Avenue on Detroit's west Side. I remember the joyous occasion with friends and family who had gathered on the enormous steps in front of the church after the couple said their wedding vows. While my cousin and her husband were greeting well-wishers, my little sister, Christine, tugged on her wedding gown and told her how pretty she looked standing proudly by her husband's side. Now that same cousin was murdered by the same man who had stood before God and man, promising to love and cherish his bride and instead had ended her life tragically with a bullet. He was tried by the court and convicted, but nothing would bring her back to the family. A link in the family chain had been tragically broken.

I attended her funeral. It was a very sad occasion. Funerals usually are. No one from my immediate family attended her funeral, but I felt compelled to pay my l respects to her. As I approached her, lying at rest, the only word that came out of my mouth was *why?* As I stood there pondering how to make sense of this tragedy, my heart ached for the woman I knew as a cousin, an educator, a wife, mother, sister, daughter, and friend. She had gone to great lengths to care for my grandmother's mental, physical, emotional, and financial needs. The last time I saw her alive was at Grandma's house. She was busy sweeping the dining-room floor, sharing with me the story of the time she had ridden a motorcycle from Detroit to Toronto with a group of people. One time, she had even taken a motorcycle trip all the way to California. The next time I saw her was at her funeral. What a strange twist of fate.

The question *why?* Would soon be answered for me personally. Little did I know that a storm was brewing in my personal life. The traumas of my past were the perfect storm for what lay ahead for me.

The traumas that I experienced had battered me emotionally. I believed that I was only good for one thing: using my body to sexually satisfy a man. I felt that the way to a man's heart was to satisfy him sexually. Misguided by this belief system, I became, in my early twenties, a victim of domestic violence.

My experience with domestic violence occurred after my cousin was murdered by her former husband. As I mourned her death, I kept wondering *Why? How could you do this to yourself, your family, to us?* I had no idea just how complex abusive relationships were.

As a child, I witnessed a physical assault on my mother that traumatized me for years. One would think that, after witnessing such an attack and after experiencing the death of my cousin, another victim of domestic abuse, I would steer clear of abusive men. Wrong. I sought them out. As a victim of sexual assault and violence, I gravitated toward domineering, abusive, and controlling men.

As a victim of sexual abuse, I believed I had done something to deserve the abuse. The abuse propelled me into a submissive role; I was attracted to dominant partners I did not know how to stand up for myself. So I settled for less and compromised myself. I became a doormat. A doormat is for wiping the filth off your feet.

I got involved with a guy who used me as his dumping ground. He didn't appreciate me at all. I hated myself, so I got involved with a guy who hated me more. I was trying to get him to love and care for me. I wanted him to complete me, love me. My level of self-esteem was nonexistent, and I was void of morals, standards, and values.

I met him at a bus stop after work one day. I looked at his outer, physical features. I thought he was cute. I wanted a boyfriend. All my friends had boyfriends; I wanted one too. I tried my best to make him love me. I had no self-esteem, no boundaries, and no self-worth. I was ripe for the picking of an abuser.

I stayed in the relationship for close to four years. Red flags were everywhere, but I chose to ignore them because I did not want to be alone. He was domineering, controlling, and mentally, verbally, and physically abusive. He cheated on me and infected me with STDs but attacked me any time I mentioned his philandering or diseases. I never cheated on him—not once—while he even tried to date my sister, friends, and cousins! I was teetering on the edge of going cuckoo.

The relationship took a turn for the worse rather quickly. I thought he loved me because he called every day at the same time (5:30 p.m.) to make sure I got home from work. I did not divert from my normal routine; I always caught the bus home. I thought he loved me and cared about my well-being, so I dismissed my mother's assessment when she told me, "He's checking on you in a controlling way."

One night I found out just how much he cared. It was a dark, rainy, cold night. He had a car, and I asked him to pick me up from work. He said he could not because his best friend's girlfriend had a medical emergency and he was on his way to the hospital to see about her. I sat at the bus stop cold, wet, hurt, and stunned. After I got home and settled in, he came over, and we had a terrible argument. We were standing at my front door, and I told him to leave. He hit me in my mouth as he turned to leave. That was the first time a man had ever hit me. I was stunned. He was getting ready to hit me again, but I slammed the door on him.

The second time he hit me, we were having an argument while I was driving. He did not have his own vehicle and I was borrowing my mother's car for our evenings out. He did not want me to drink, and I had had several drinks that night. I was trying to take a stance, and he knocked me in the head and jumped out the car and ran. I figured out he was headed to a bus stop, so I flagged down a police officer. The officer went right to him at the bus stop and questioned him. I sat in the police car at a distance. But I took him back just as my mother took her abuser back.

The next time he attempted to hit me, I was standing against a brick building. We had been arguing, and he drew back his fist to hit me; I closed my eyes real tight, because I knew, if my head hit the building, I was probably going to die. Only this time, he stopped, walked away, got into his car, and sped away.

After a series of breakups and make-ups, the turning point came after he infected me with a sexually transmitted disease for the third time. I had had it with the humiliation, with the embarrassment of going to the doctor about these problems; I was finished with him. He did not take it well. I had just purchased a brand-new car, and it became the target of vandalism. First a brick was thrown through the windshield. I got that fixed. Then two of my tires were flattened. The grand finale was when a can of yellow paint was thrown on the hood of my bright red car. I could never prove who did it. I did have to leave my home and stay with friends and relatives out of fear that the attacks would escalate. He followed me to work. I had to notify my employer about the abusive relationship and park as close to the building as possible for safety reasons.

Hiding from my ex was taking an emotional toll on me. I did not want to end up like my cousin who had died at the hands of her ex-husband. One day while at work, I was having a telephone conversation about my domestic situation. I was crying and discussing my fear of becoming a victim. I did not know my female coworker was listening. After I hung up the phone, she—without mentioning the details of the telephone conversation that she had apparently listened to—told me to read Psalms 35—a petition for God's intervention. Psalms 35 is extensive, but I will share a portion:

1 Plead my cause, O Lord, with them that strive with me; fight against them that fight against me:

2 Take hold of shield and buckler, and stand up for mine help.

3 Draw out also the spear, and stop the way against them that persecute me: say unto my soul, "I am thy salvation."

4 Let them be confounded and put to shame that seek after my soul: let them be turned back and brought to confusion that devise my hurt.

5 Let them be as chaff before the wind: and let the angel of the Lord chase them.

6 Let their way be dark and slippery: and let the anger of the Lord persecute them.

7 For without cause have they hid their net in a pit, which without cause they have digged for my soul.

8 Let destruction come upon him at unawares; and let his net that he hath hid catch himself: into that very destruction let him fall.

9 And my soul shall be joyful in the Lord: it shall rejoice in his salvation (Psalms 35:1–9).

This prayer was a comfort to me. I knew my situation was more than my family, friends, and I could handle.

It was only after the breakup that I began to see the signs that had been there all along. Out of desperation for companionship, I approached him. He did not approach me. I made the first move. In our four-year relationship, we went to dinner one time. I gave him money, borrowed my mother's and sister's cars to drive us around to outings at the park and to the movies. He always looked at other women during these outings. Almost as soon as we started dating, he let me know that he wanted to talk to my sister—and not just to say hello and how are you. I begged him not to leave me when he tried. I told him I was lonely, fat, and ugly; and nobody wanted me, and that I needed him. From that moment on, he treated me like dirt, and I tried everything in my power to make things right. I wanted him to love me. Sadly, I had no clue as to what love was. I did not know how to date or court. I did not know how to be wooed. I had a fantasy of what romance was supposed to be—the kind of romance I had seen in movies or read in books. I did not have a blueprint for male-female relationships. Daddy was gone. No one ever filled his shoes.

One summer day, long after the relationship ended, I was on my way to the store and stopped briefly to talk to a guy from the neighborhood, a childhood friend of mine, when, suddenly, my ex-boyfriend drove by and glared at me. I had moved on with my life. I had lost weight, made new friends, and enjoyed life without him—so what did I care? Let him glare!

My sister had just come home, saw my ex-boyfriend driving around the neighborhood and became concerned. She said she had an eerie feeling about me that day—that, as I walked down the street to the store, I had an eerie cloud or aura around me. She was frightened.

I made my purchase at the store and was just leaving the building when my ex-boyfriend appeared and confronted me. He was getting ready to say or do something, and I ran back in the store. Suddenly, my sister and her male friend pulled up and got out of the car. My sister's friend began arguing with my ex, and a large crowd gathered around. They both yelled at each other, but no one threw the first punch. One of the onlookers attempted to steal my ex's car, so he ran to his vehicle, jumped in, and pulled off. God used my sister to save my life that day. I believe my ex was going to hurt or kill me that day.

To put an end to the relationship with my former boyfriend, I hired a lawyer and went to court before a judge with my complaint of abuse and stalking perpetrated by my former boyfriend. The judge sided with me and ordered him to stay away from me, period. After our court date, he tried one more time to resurrect the relationship by sending a letter to me pleading with me to take him back. I sent the letter to my lawyer. I never heard from him again.

CHAPTER 5

Oh, Happy Day!

AS A CHILD, I was the only one in my household who woke up to go to church on Sunday mornings. There was a Baptist church in the next block. On Sunday mornings, I would walk to church, greet the ushers, and make my way to balcony, where I would sit, held in awe by the service. The spirit of the Lord moved in that church. I sat in the balcony, watching the nurses in their white uniforms, white shoes, and white stockings tend to the parishioners who were overcome with the Holy Spirit. I would giggle as the women danced clean out of their big hats and into the aisles when the spirit was high. I went to Vacation Bible School, and I visited storefront churches in my neighborhood, while I endured the trauma in my childhood. I even participated in summer programs run by Catholic nuns. It was there where I first learned the song, "If I Had a Hammer." I can still remember a nun playing joyfully on her guitar as the children and I sang in chorus.

I found peace in the house and presence of God. When I was a child, God was laying the spiritual foundation of the calling he had upon my life.

Before I formed thee in the belly I knew thee; and before

thou camest forth out of the womb I sanctified thee, and I ordained thee a prophet unto the nations. (Jeremiah 1:5)

At a young age, I already had it in my heart to help the hurting and the poor. During the holiday season, my elementary school hosted a canned-food drive; each child was asked to bring a canned good for needy families. Concerned that families would not have a good holiday, I brought several canned goods.

As an adult, I continued for years in my vicious cycle of engaging in short-lived relationships until, one day, my sister, Christine, invited me to church. Christine had recently joined a local church, and I noticed the transformation in her immediately. She had recently ended an abusive relationship and, through the prompting of a family friend, had begun attending church.

The weekend my sister invited me to church was the same weekend I had a sexual tryst. I drove to his home after midnight and had a terrible accident with my car. It was amazing I survived. So I was reluctant to go to services at first because of my activities that weekend—drinking heavily, hanging out with a male friend, and getting involved in an auto accident (talk about a trifecta!)—but Christine said I could come to church and worship the Lord just as I was, so I took her up on her offer.

The Lord hath appeared of old unto me, saying, "Yea, I have loved thee with an everlasting love: therefore with lovingkindness have I drawn thee. (Jeremiah 31:3).

Except for attending weddings, funerals, confirmations, and baptisms, I had not been in a church in years. Prior to attending that Sunday-morning service, I had attended a church service with my cousin. My cousin was fresh out of college, and I was excited for her. She was making her mark in the world. She had pledged a sorority, traveled, and surrounded herself with positive people. She had her own car and apartment. She had a nice, respectful boyfriend who treated me like a sister. Once in my despair over dating my abusive boyfriend, I asked my cousin if her boyfriend every called her the "B" word. My cousin's answer was no. She said they argued sometime, but he never called her a female dog. My boyfriend called me every foul name in the book.

My cousin did not drink or smoke; she chose a path that proved to be fruitful. At one point, her job required her to travel—a lot. My emotions were mixed. I was happy for my cousin, and yet I was sad because my life was in the dumps. Deep down inside, I knew I missed the "boat" when I was dismissed from college. One of my heart's desires was to travel for my job too.

I was spending the weekend with her to get a rest from my abusive boyfriend. That Sunday morning she invited me to her church. As the organist played and sang a beautiful song, tears began to fall from my eyes. In my state of brokenness, God was moving me with his spirit, but I didn't realize or accept this as yet; I was still trying to do it on my own. I tried to stop drinking on my own. I tried to stop engaging in the abusive relationship on my own. I tried to put the drugs down on my own, but I could not do it. For some reason, I thought I had to "dress up" for God or to be presentable in order to enter into his presence. I believed I had to clean myself up before I came to God because of my lifestyle. But he welcomed me just the way I was—brokenhearted, wounded, hurt, and dealing with the pain of my past. God showered me with his love on me that Sunday morning. This was the beginning of great things to come.

> And he arose, and came to his father. But when he was yet a great way off, his father saw him, and had compassion, and ran, and fell on his neck, and kissed him. And the son said unto him, "Father, I have sinned against heaven, and in thy sight, and am no more worthy to be called thy son." But the father said to his servants, "Bring forth the best robe, and put it on him, and put a ring on his hand, and shoes

on his feet: And bring hither the fatted calf, and kill it; and let us eat, and be merry: For this my son was dead, and is alive again; he was lost, and is found." And they began to be merry. (Luke 15:20–24)

Like the prodigal son, even though I had distanced myself from Christ with riotous living, drinking, smoking and men, God saw me coming to church on that Sunday morning to Unity Cathedral of Faith and welcomed me with arms opened wide. With cigarette smoke on my breath, alcohol in my system, and the smell of a man on my skin, Christ had spoken to my situation that Sunday morning over the pulpit, and he wanted me just the way I *was*.

I do not recall the message that was preached that morning, but I remember exactly what occurred at altar call. Prior to attending that Sunday morning service, I read the story about how Jesus called Lazarus forth from the grave.

> 39 Jesus saith, "Take ye away the stone." Martha the sister of him that was dead, saith unto him, "Lord, by this time he stinketh: for he hath be dead four days."

> 40 Jesus saith unto her, "Said I not unto thee, that, if thou wouldest believe, thou shouldest see the glory of God?"

> 41 Then they took away the stone from the place where the dead was laid. And Jesus lifted up his eyes, and said, "Father, I thank thee that thou hast heard me.

> 42 "And I knew that thou hearest me always: but because the people which stand by I said it, that they may believe that thou hast sent me."

> 43 And when he thus has spoken, he cried with a loud voice, "Lazarus, come forth."

> 44 And he that was dead came forth, bound hand and foot

with graveclothes: and face was bound about with a napkin. Jesus saith unto them, "Loose him and let him go." (John 11:39–44)

I mouthed the words, "Father, I know you hear me." I mouthed the words to that scripture as I walked to the altar. I kept repeating that prayer, as Bishop Clarence B. Haddon looked down, smiling on me from the pulpit, I kept reciting it. It was time to walk in victory. It was time to drop the chains of defeat and depression, to loose, and to let me go. Everything that had me bound and chained had to let go. Every lie the devil told had to lose its grip and stronghold on me that morning. Notice in verse 44, Jesus was telling every demon to let *go*! Once I reached the altar, Prophetess Joyce Haddon laid hands on me, and the power of God fell on me; and I fell on the floor.

Like Jeremiah said, it is like fire shut up in my bones. I knew God was real and his love for me was real. I was crying my eyes out, lying out on the floor at the front of the church. The spirit of the Lord knocked me out. It started at my feet and rushed to my head, and I fell out, and God took control. Shortly after, the ministers ushered me into a room and began to pray, and I started speaking in tongues as tears fell from my eyes. All my senses were keen; I was in a room with two ministers ushering in the presence of the Lord. The sun was shining through the window. I was on my knees saying, "Jesus, Jesus, Jesus!"—and Jesus showed up! I was speaking in an unknown tongue as tears flowed from my eyes. I will always remember the warmth and peace I felt that day. I wanted more.

I learned Jesus had been waiting for me all those years when I denied him, like the prodigal son, who left the presence of God. His son, Jesus, who atoned for my sins, welcomed me that morning with arms opened wide! I felt so loved and so free. Later that night, I returned to service, and, during the service, I was caught up in the Holy Spirit, like the women I saw in the church when I was a child. It was like the book of Acts—and, like a mighty rushing wind, the Holy Ghost fell upon me, and I danced in the aisles of the church. It is the dance of all dances. Baby, I was gone. Dancing, and crying for the Lord. I had the dance partner of all dance partners that night. He chose me. He rushed to me. God picked me to *dance*! Believe me, when God steps in, *everything* changes for the better. God gives you better benefits, better health, a better life, and a better future. Everything is better. If it is not better, it is a lie, and only Satan can tell lies.

Oh, what a feeling! I immediately joined Unity Cathedral of Faith and attended on a regular basis. One of my prayers to the Father in Jesus' name was to allow my mother to live to see me become a better person mentally, physically, emotionally, spiritually, and financially. Over the course of the years, Momma had seen the worst of the worst in me: the drunken nights, the abusive relationships, and the suicide attempts. My prayer was that she would live to see the best in me.

Keep in mind, Satan will try you because no abuser wants you to be free. My last suicide attempt was in December of 1992. I remember that month so well because I had given my life to the Lord and was filled with the Holy Spirit. I was depressed because it was the holiday season, and my fifteen-year-old collie Prince was stricken with arthritis. He was dying. I did not want to let him go. I had a fistful of Tylenol in one hand and a glass of water in the other. With tears in my eyes, I lifted the Tylenol to my mouth, and suddenly I began to speak in tongues. I threw the pills away. That was my last attempt. I thank God for the blood!

Being a "babe" in Christ, I was new to the scriptures. Everything was new to me. Over the years, I had heard scriptures, but I never studied them for myself. One night, a friend who was in Christ had a birthday celebration. The theme of her birthday was printed on a big banner in the front of the banquet room, and it read, "Delight thyself also in the Lord, and he shall give thee the desires of thine heart" (Psalms 37:4).

That scripture pricked *my* heart. I kept reading it and wrote it down so I could go home and highlight it in my Bible. I grabbed hold of that scripture and never let go. I was excited by the thought that God wanted to give me the desires of my heart after everything I had done.

The most pressing desire of my heart was to return to Marygrove College and finish what I had started. It had been close to ten years since my dismissal from the college, and life without a college education or training had proven to be economically challenging. I was working two jobs to make one decent income. One night, fatigued, while working my second job in retail; I remember looking around the department store at the employees, the customers, and the kids, and I came to a conclusion: *I cannot do this anymore. I have to go back to school.* Like the four lepers, I had two choices: one was to stay here and work two jobs and never know what could have been; the other was to step out in faith, and start the process of going back to school to finish what I started. I called the college and asked what I had to do to reapply. I was given the criteria needed to reapply. Like the four lepers, I got up and started walking.

My interest in social work came into being one night during a church service. I was an usher at the time, and one of the ushers was a social worker, who would tell me about her job and responsibilities working with young people. It sounded intriguing. Every time she talked about her job, it reminded me of how miserable I was with my job. On this particular night, she told me her organization was hiring. I sprang up from my seat and asked, "Where do I apply?" She politely informed me that I needed a bachelor's or master's degree in social work. My heart sank! I knew then that my dream was not going to be realized overnight, but the wheels had been put in motion.

I continued to read the *Michigan Chronicle* weekly. I read the classified at my desk because, through faith, I was going to become a social worker one day. As I said, I did not become a social worker overnight. It was a process. My degrees would not, by some miracle, fall into my lap or come knocking on my door. I had to pursue them. I think about the man who lay by the pool of Bethesda for over thirty years, waiting for the angel to stir the water so that he could be healed. At the appointed season, the angel would come and stir the water, and someone would jump up, run to the water, and be healed! Finally Jesus came by and asked the man "Will thou be made whole?" and this man gave Jesus a million reasons why he could not make it to the water: "My back; my head; these people keep taking cuts all the while I'm lying here, waiting for someone to get my healing. I keep yelling, 'Hey, buddy, can you get me to the water?'"

We make too many excuses about why we cannot reach our dreams! I wanted to finish what I started by moving in the direction I wanted to go!

CHAPTER 6

The Desires of Thine Heart

Delight thyself also in the Lord; and He shall
give thee the desires of thine heart.

—Psalms 37:4

GOD IS TRULY a God of another chance. My chance came one glorious Sunday morning during praise and worship service at Unity Cathedral of Faith, the church where I had surrendered my life to Christ after a night of drinking, smoking, and boyfriend. I spotted a fellow parishioner praising the Lord with her arms flung wide. As I looked closer, I noticed a beautiful Kente cloth resting on her shoulders and a graduation cap and tassel sitting like a crown upon her head. The bright yellow, green, black, white, and red colors of the Kente cloth were striking. I was in awe of the Kente cloth. I kept my eyes on her throughout the service because I did not want her to leave before I had the opportunity to investigate her glorious attire. I wanted to know its meaning, so I approached her after the service. I learned she was graduating from the same college I had attended, Marygrove, with a bachelor's degree in social work. The Kente cloth was an emblem of the Association of Black Social Workers (student chapter), of which she was a member. My first thought was *I have to have it! I have to have that Kente cloth.* I was not even thinking about the degree required to earn the Kente cloth. God used that Kente cloth as a catalyst to jump-start me into getting my college degree. Believe me; God has an awesome way of getting you where you need to go.

The desire of my heart was to finish what I started years earlier at Marygrove College: to obtain my college degree. To re-enroll, I would have to submit a letter of petition pleading my case for re-entry to the Marygrove College academic-review board, which only met once a year in May to consider the reinstatement of former students who had been dismissed from the college. I had to explain why I believed I should be considered and what I had achieved academically during my absence from the college that warranted consideration to be readmitted. It was already the month of May, so, believe it or not, I had just one week to submit my typewritten petition detailing why I should be readmitted. God worked it out in my favor. My mother typed my letter of petition and we proofread the petition aloud. I received a letter from the college academic-review board stating my acceptance into Marygrove College would be dependent upon my transcript from Wayne County Community College, the college I had attended years before in order to make up the classes I had failed at Marygrove College— the same college I had excelled in academically when I was there. I knew I could do the work! I was able to transfer several credits from Wayne County Community College to Marygrove as a result. When you hang on to your dreams, God will give you double for your trouble:

> For your shame ye shall have double; and for confusion they shall rejoice in their portion: therefore in their land they shall possess the double; everlasting joy shall be unto them. (Isaiah 61:7)

> Instead of your [former] shame you shall have a twofold recompense; instead of dishonor and reproach [your people] shall rejoice in their portion. Therefore in their land they shall possess double [what they had forfeited]; everlasting joy shall be theirs. (Isaiah 61:7, Amplified)

I returned to Marygrove College in the fall of 1993 on academic probation. My GPA was 1.7. That was my GPA when I was dismissed in 1982. As a return student, I excelled. I hit the books hard. Initially, I began my college career by taking two classes in the evening while working full-time at the bank. The process of returning to school was a process. Gradually, I worked my way up to three classes and then four or full-time. I would spend hours in the school and public library. I joined study groups. I aligned myself with classmates who wanted to excel academically. I pulled all-nighters. I kept the coffee pot brewing. With the support of my family, I went from working full-time to part-time so that I could complete my student internship. I was determined to do well in math. I selected math teachers who were passionate about math and went the extra distance with their students. I had one math teacher who met with the class on Saturday mornings! Talk about commitment! I was there bright-eyed and bushy-tailed. I began to embrace math because it challenged me mentally. I had to work parts of my brain that had been dormant as the result of a drug-and-alcohol-induced haze. I passed Algebra I and II and Geometry I and II with A's and B's due to long nights of studying, tutoring, and sacrifice. I passed physics, statistics and biology with A and B grades due to long nights of studying and sacrifice.

These were the same classes I failed when I first entered the college as a teen. I failed because I did not want to go through the process. I chose that easy route of giving up and quitting.

This time around, the college experience was beautiful. I had the faith, but I had to apply my faith by going though the steps or process. I applied for financial aid and student loans. I formed relationships with students who, like me, were determined to earn their college degree. (I learned they had life stories too.) Failing any class was not an option. I was in the fight of my life. My family was my cheering section and my support system, and I did not want to let anyone down. I even had the prayers and support of my spiritual leaders, Bishop Clarence Haddon and Prophetess Joyce Haddon. I was on a mission. I studied day and night. I cut off the television, limited my telephone conversations with the exception of those with my study partners. I stopped partying and drinking and dropped my boyfriends. I studied wherever I went; I was studying when I took my car to get an oil change. One time, I took Mom for an outpatient procedure; I had my books with me. The doctor was impressed. After he told me Mom was okay, he asked about my classes and wished me well.

I made up all the classes that I had failed. My GPA soared. My confidence and self-esteem soared! After I was released from academic probation, I had to declare a major. With a 2.4 GPA, I did not qualify for the teaching program. So, although I had the desire to teach, I declared social work as my major.

Great choice! I never looked back. The Marygrove College Social Work Program was a wonderful experience. I loved every aspect of social work. I loved helping people, healing people, and lending a hand to those whom society overlooked. I continued to excel academically, eventually exceeding the 2.7 GPA requirements for teaching, but I embraced the social-work program and continued with social work as my major.

Like the prophet Daniel, the spirit of excellence was upon me. I assumed the role of leadership as I advanced in my college career. I was selected to introduce renowned Harvard professor Dr. Cornell West at a speaking engagement hosted by the University of Detroit Mercy. He had just published his new book, *Restoring Hope*. Prior to Dr. West's lecture, I had lunch with him and a host of city leaders, community leaders, ministers, and college professors. After lunch we were escorted to the college auditorium. The auditorium was at capacity. A student rushed into the auditorium and said all entrances to the college were jammed. Cars were backing up on the main street, Livernois. People were coming from everywhere! My mother and sister came to hear my brief introduction for the guest speaker, Dr. West, but they were unable to get in because of the heavy traffic.

Upon returning to Marygrove College, I was walking through Madame Cadillac Hall on campus and noted an event was going on in one of the formal dining rooms. The ladies were adorned in blue and white sashes. I was intrigued. I walked in and asked a student about the sashes. There is something about me and sashes. I was told the sashes represented Phi Alpha, a national student social-work honor society, and the event was a membership drive. At the time, I did not meet the criteria for admittance because I was still on academic probation. But, after my grades improved and I was released from academic probation, not only did I join Phi Alpha but eventually became president of the society! In addition, I became a member of the Association of Black Social Workers (Student Chapter) and of Network (a social-work organization), and, in 1997, I was voted Student Social Worker of the Year. I received an Iota Gamma Award for outstanding service in the community. Collectively, the social-work organizations hosted bake sales to aid and assist women and children housed in Interim House, a domestic-violence shelter in Detroit at Christmas, flood victims in Kentucky, and students in need of food and financial assistance. The social-work organizations were awesome. As a student intern during my undergraduate studies, I was responsible for the implementation of the Hamtramck Harvest, a food program in Hamtramck, MI.

As a student intern, I realized that Detroit, Michigan, and Highland Park, Michigan, had food programs to assist the poor and needy in those cities, while the city of Hamtramck, MI did not. I brought this to the attention of my field placement supervisor, Reverend Sharon Buttry, who was intrigued with the idea and wanted *me* to meet with the food-program director and his assistant. She contacted the Family Independence Agency, and the director came out to the agency to meet with me! I could not believe it when I saw Reverend Buttry standing back like a proud momma while I stated my case! The food program was implemented. It is still in operation today.

Graduating Magna Cum Laude, adorned in my graduation cap and gown, Association of Black Social Workers Kente cloth, Blue and White Phi Alpha sash, and a gold Network Medallion, I was nominated and selected as the commencement speaker for the Marygrove College graduating class of 1998!

In the spring of 1999, I earned my master's degree in social work from Wayne State University after completing the accelerated program. As a graduate of Wayne State University, I attended *three* graduation ceremonies. One ceremony was for social workers only. One ceremony was for graduates of the National Association of Black Social Workers, student chapter. The last ceremony was the grand finale: the graduation for all graduates at Cobo Center in Downtown Detroit. I danced my way into the Cobo Center Auditorium! I got my "happy dance" on!

My grandmother's death sparked a chain of events that forever changed my life. Her death brought a group of middle-aged cousins together around a kitchen table to contemplate our lives over a round of drinks one lazy afternoon. I could have chosen to believe that at thirty-something years old, my life was indeed over. Instead, I opted to dismiss my cousin's rationalization that we would never be greater by setting out to disprove what he believed and achieving, via opposition to his discontent, the seemingly impossible through sheer determination. I moved forward and declared victory over my circumstances. Yes, in the end, through God's grace, my actions spoke louder than his words!

By God's grace, I have experienced the desires of my heart. I shook off the thought of making big money and rolled up my sleeves to become a first responder to individuals who have suffered trauma. I am a shoulder to lean on. I am a shoulder to cry on. I visit individuals in their time of need, wherever they are—in their homes, in hospital rooms, courtrooms, schools, shelters, and treatment centers. In homes I have visited, I have stepped on cockroaches that were getting too close for comfort. I have driven past drug dealers selling their wares on street corners. I have walked in on sex acts and drug deals. I drove fast out of neighborhoods when gunshots went off and witnessed fights between family members. The money I have made has afforded me the ability to pay my tithes and offerings and my bills, with something left over for quality time with family and friends. I have traveled to places I have always wanted to see. I have shopped in New York, Chicago, Los Angeles, and other cities during my travels in the United States and abroad. (I am still working on my desire to go to Paris and Africa for my shopping excursions.) I have attending meetings in the Coleman A. Young Municipal Building on behalf of my job with the Alzheimer's Association. As a social-work professional and grief and loss counselor, I have attended hearings and trials in 36th District Court and Frank Murphy Hall of Justice on behalf of individuals and families. These are the same buildings I walked through in faith with my red Coach briefcase while I worked the switchboard at the bank.

Years ago, my neighborhood was surrounded by vacant lots. Sometimes the grass would grow as tall as me. I would drown out the city noise by playing soft, soothing music. As a matter of fact, I lived next-door to a grassy vacant lot. Sometimes, while sitting on my front porch, I would sit back and close my eyes and envision myself on a huge cruise ship sailing in the middle of a big blue-green ocean to an unknown destination. Reclining in my lawn chair—instead of grass, asphalt streets, blurring music from passing cars, vacant lots, and tall grass—I was surrounded by a vast blue-green ocean, listening to a calypso band in my swimsuit, flip flops, big sunglasses, and a big floppy straw hat, lounging in the sun on the deck with a cool drink.

In 1999, after graduating with my master's degree in social work from Wayne State University, I went on my first seven-day cruise to Montego Bay, Grand Cayman Island, and Cozumel, Mexico, aboard the *Carnival*

Celebration cruise ship. Several classmates and I treated ourselves for a job well done. We spent the night in New Orleans. I had never been to New Orleans and believed it was only fun during the Mardi gras celebration. I was so wrong. We had a blast in New Orleans. We celebrated the food, the music, the street cars, and the shopping. I was amazed. I refused to show my bra, however, to people on the balconies beckoning me with beads. We walked along Bourbon Street that night, had a great dinner of fried oysters, Po-boys, and red beans and rice.

Before sailing out the next morning to our exotic islands, we toured the French Quarter and had a breakfast—samplings of chicory coffee, pralines, and beignets. We followed up by shopping at a flea market. The first night on the ship was absolutely amazing. We laughed so hard to the point of intoxication. Our small group shared two cabins, and we staged a contest by decorating our cabins. It was a blast.

On the morning I arrived in Montego Bay, I woke up, looked out of the cabin porthole, and was astounded by what I saw. The ship had already docked, and I thought my eyes were playing tricks on me. I was still groggy, so I asked my roommate, "What is that?" With a big smile, she said, "Girl, those are islands!"

I was in awe! I went from the front porch to the ports of Montego Bay, Jamaica, Cozumel, Mexico, and Grand Cayman Islands! I have been on two other cruises since that time! Nassau, Key West, Paradise Island, Bahamas! Not to mention Chicago; New York; Nappanee Indian (Amish Acres); Niagara Falls; Florida (Palm Beach, Miami, Fort Lauderdale, and Sarasota); New Orleans; Seattle, Washington; Los Angeles; Kansas; Atlanta; Fifth Avenue (New York), Worth Avenue (Palm Beach) and Put-In-Bay, Ohio.

I had always wanted to go to Martha's Vineyard. Mom and I would go to a seafood restaurant on Saturday afternoons for lunch. We would always sit in our favorite booth by a huge fish tank, and I would order the Martha's Vineyard salad, believing by faith I would get there one day. In the spring of 2008, I took a trip to Massachusetts and visited Cape Cod, Martha' Vineyard, Provincetown, and Plymouth—all my favorite places.

Once we arrived at the Massachusetts state line, we found a restaurant that served Lobster Rolls. I could not stop eating the lobster and scallop rolls! God even went over and above my desires with added extras—for example, while we were visiting Cape Cod, the tide rolled back, exposing the ocean floor. I stood on the ocean floor spinning around with joy. The ocean's floor!

While visiting Seattle, Washington, I was able to visit Pike Street. Pike Street was amazing: fresh fish everywhere. I wanted to send home a crate of everything—fresh clams, crab legs, lobsters, and shrimp. While there, I visited a beautiful, serene Japanese-inspired garden. Everything was so green and lush. I could have stayed in that garden forever.

I am so glad I got up from the kitchen table of despair and pressed forward by faith. I made the decision to get off my do-nothing self and do something to change my future into something extraordinary. Prior to writing this book, I submitted a brief article to *Essence* magazine for the "Get Lifted" column. The article was the basis for *The Desires of Thine Heart*. I was hopeful that my article would be selected, but it was not. I checked the mail and my email daily. Eventually, I took that 1300-word article and expanded it into a book! Never give up!

As I continue to delight myself in the Lord, the Lord continues to give me the desires of my heart. I have developed a "Desires of Thine Heart" folder. In the folder, I place photos of the places I would like to visit, things I would want to do, foods I would want to eat, the car that I would want to own, the home that I would like to live in, and projects that I would like to complete. I place the pictures in a folder or put photos on my wall. As I achieve my desires, I remove the pictures from the folder or take them off the wall. All the while, I keep adding: If my heart's desire can take me from my front porch to the ports of the Caribbean Sea, the desires of my heart can take me anywhere!

CHAPTER 7

Forgive and F-O-R-G-E-T!

THE ACT OF forgiveness has been instrumental in my life. I had the ability to hold a grudge and hate for years. I was consumed with unforgiving until, by God's grace, I learned to let go and let God.

My mother had no knowledge of the sexual abuse I suffered. I never said a word. To be honest, I cannot remember if the truth was ever disclosed during any treatments I had as a child. I told my mother the truth in my adult years. For some strange reason, I had this notion that my offender was going to make it right, come clean, apologize, compensate me, and give me back what he had stolen. I remember the time I went bowling with my friend and her brother, my offender. I remember him chastising me in front of other bowlers, and I wanted to scream, "How dare you speak to me that way after what you have done to me!" For some strange reason, I was expecting him to treat me better. After all, he had violated me, and I was keeping the secret. Surely he was going to make it right. At least, that is what I thought. As I grew and matured and was able to process what took place, that seed he planted grew into hatred. I hated him for years. I mean H-A-T-E-D. I wanted him to suffer as I had suffered. I wanted him to apologize publicly. For years, I mourned my childhood. I was unforgiving of him. As

I grew older, I avoided him at all cost. We avoided mentioning his name in our home. We walked softly around the issue of the sexual abuse. It was as if not talking about it made it go away, as if it did not happen. I became bitter, angry, and filled with rage. I turn my anger, rage, and bitterness inward. I was my own worst enemy.

One day, out of sheer frustration, I asked my mother the burning question, "Why won't he apologize to me?"

Staring me straight in the eyes, she said, "The devil will never apologize for anything." That is when I began to put things into perspective.

Ephesians 6:12 says, "For we wrestle not against flesh and blood but against principalities, against powers, against the rulers of the darkness of the world, against spiritual wickedness in high places." After meditating on this scripture, I realized there was a demonic spirit attached to my offender, yet I hated him. I hated what I could see of him with my naked eye, but there was something more sinister going on inside of him, using him to wound, bruise, and violate me. My guess is that someone violated him, and that is how sin entered into him. The enemy does not discriminate; he will use anyone who has a weak link in their armor. My deep hatred for him was destroying me mentally and physically.

There is a saying, "Not forgiving is like drinking poison and expecting that the person whom you won't forgive will die." This proved to be true for me. Yes, I was violated; and, yes, I believed my offender deserved to be punished, but to be unforgiving was destroying me. Not to forgive is *not* God's will! God's will is to forgive those who persecute us! Because I did not forgive him, I suffered, and I suffered a lot. My emotions channeled into anger, bitterness, rage, and resentment. My life was spiraling out of control. I can only imagine how many blessings and healings were blocked because of my lack of forgiveness. As a Christian, I learned some hard lessons about the inability to forgive. Prayers went unanswered. Favor was withheld. I prayed for a healing, but I did not get healed. Had I forgiven my offender, there is a possibility my prayers would have reached heaven, and God would have heard my prayer and healed me. My affliction got progressively worse. I had "tied" God's hands in this matter.

The book of Matthew 18:23–35 makes a poignant statement about the consequences when you don't forgive:

> 23 Therefore the kingdom of heaven is like a human king who wished to settle accounts with his attendant.
>
> 24 When he began the accounting, one was brought to him who owed him 10, 000 talents [probably about $10,000,000].
>
> 25 And because he could not pay, his master ordered him to be sold, with his wife and his children and everything that he possessed, and payments to be made.
>
> 26 So the attendant fell on his knees, begging him, "Have patience with me, and I will pay you everything."
>
> 27 And his master's heart was moved with compassion, and he released him and forgave him [i.e., canceled] the debt.
>
> 28 But that same attendant, as he went out, found one of his fellow servants who owed a hundred denarii [about twenty dollars]; and he caught him by the throat and said, "Pay what you owe!"
>
> 29 So his fellow attendant fell down and begged him earnestly, "Give me time, and I will pay you all!"
>
> 30 But he was unwilling, and he went out and had him put in prison till he should pay the debt.
>
> 31 When his fellow attendants saw what had happened, they were greatly distressed, and they went and told everything that had taken place to their master.

32 Then his master called him and said to him, "You contemptible and wicked attendant! I forgave and cancelled all that [great] debt of yours because you begged me to.

33 "And should you not have had pity and mercy on your fellow attendant, as I had pity and mercy on you?"

34 And in wrath his master turned him over to the tortures [the jailers, tormentors], till he should pay all that he owed.

35 So also my heavenly Father will deal with every one of you if you do not freely forgive your brother from your heart his offenses (The Amplified Bible).

Noah Webster's *American Dictionary of the English Language* (1828) defines *torment* as follows:

- to put to extreme pain or anguish
- to inflict excruciating pain and misery either of body or mind
- to pain; to distress
- Extreme pain, anguish to the utmost degree
- to tease, to vex, to harass with petty annoyances

Tormentor is defined as "he or that which torments, one who inflicts penal anguish or tortures." To be painfully honest, I was miserable because I vehemently refused to forgive my offenders; I actually surrendered my power over to them. I woke up hating them in the morning, and I laid my head down on the pillow at night hating them. My hatred had me bound and wrapped like a mummy. I was swaddled in mental, emotional, and physical torment.

Forgiveness must come from the heart, genuinely; God is really big on forgiveness. Forgiveness is an immediate act of the heart. Trust, on the other hand, may take a while. Forgive yourself for your mistakes, bad choices, bad decisions, and bad relationships. Forgive your childhood pain and walk to the light of love, forgiveness, and restoration. You cannot change your past, but you can navigate or chart the course of a bright future beyond your dreams, thoughts, goals, and desires.

Not forgiving will cause a host of problems—mentally, physically, emotionally, and spiritually. Lack of forgiveness and torment go hand in hand. Think of these two culprits as the buddy system with a mission to annihilate. June Newman Davis, author of *Scripture Keys Power Manual*, dedicated an entire chapter to lack of forgiveness and the benefits and blessings in forgiveness. I will share a powerful revelation she wrote on how the state of unforgiving attacks the physical body.

Unforgiveness will engender hate, vengeance, anger, and murder. All the spirits aforementioned give the enemy the ground to bring arthritis, bone diseases (blood diseases), bursitis (Pr. 12:25), colitis, spastic bowel, gallstones, kidney stones, migraines, hypertension, ulcers, cancer and early death. Medicine has proved through research that 98% of the diseases in the human body came from emotional shock, trauma, and unforgiveness or grudges. These hurts, offenses, criticisms, and persecutions cause deep wounds and bring about chemical changes in our natural bodies, thus provoking many diseases. The Lord knew how our physical body would react to these traumas and then how Satan would take advantage of us (2 Co. 2:10–11), so He gave a way to pour His healing balm over these wounds through the act of forgiveness. Forgiveness is divine medicine!

Here is a checklist to determine if you are walking in a state of not forgiving:

- Do you have a compulsion to tell others what has been perpetrated upon you, sometimes (or all the time) naming people and events?

- Are you always blurting out of your mouth this information without really wanting to, what so-and-so did and said?
- Do you still resent what someone said or did, even after they have asked your forgiveness?
- Can you forget what they did and the harm they perpetrated upon you and your loved ones?
- Do you avoid this person in every way you can?
- Are you uncomfortable in their presence?
- Are you affected physically?
- Are you affected mentally?
- Do you want them to get their payback or what is due them?

If you checked one or more of these items, chances are you are suffering from a lack of forgiveness. Now ask yourself, is not forgiving worth your physical health? Does your failing health affect the person or persons you have not forgiven?

Not forgiving is a blessing/favor/breakthrough blocker because it disconnects our power surge to God. Not forgiving will result in hatred, bitterness, resentment, fear, anger, jealousy, envy, grudge, and rage. I call this sludge because, if this lack of forgiveness goes unchecked and there is no resolve, the sludge forms and becomes pungent. The blessing blocker gains strength and opens the door to more sludge. Take a look below:

- hatred hardens
- bitterness stagnates
- fear paralyzes
- anger weakens
- jealousy deadens
- envy consumes
- grudge builds resentment
- rage equals violence

Not forgiving is a ticking time bomb. You become consumed with it—the sludge symptoms—and you cannot hear from God, and God cannot hear from you. Being disconnected from God is dangerous. Lack of forgiveness is a sin. Praying for and forgiving our offenders is a gateway to healing mentally, physically, emotionally, and spiritually. We reap tremendous benefits when we forgive and forget any and everybody who has wronged us, caused us pain and trauma. I just surrendered and gave it over to God. I forgave my offender(s).

I have learned forgiveness is immediate but that building trust takes time. I have heard people say, "I will forgive, but I will not forget." Trust me; such people are only hurting themselves. If you do not forget, you will keep remembering, and that is like throwing salt in the wound or continually peeling back the scab that is trying to heal. That wound is going to become infected, and anything infected is going require serious attention. Just as life goes on, people move on too, and here you are stuck in a valley of torment and lack of forgiveness. Essentially you are stagnated. Stagnated things are not productive. Nothing grows in them. Like standing water, they develop a foul odor and become a dumping ground for pollutants to fester in and rot. Nobody wants to keep company with something stinking, rotting, and decaying. If you do not believe me, try sitting with rotting cheese or spoiled milk. You are going to hightail it out of there.

Another way to look at lack of forgiveness is like this: If you are a pipe out of which water flows, not forgiving will block your spiritual flow. Not forgiving will cause sludge to build up, stopping the natural flow of things such as your healing, gifts, blessings, and talents. I have known people to develop aneurysms, cancers, heart diseases, and a host of other sicknesses and diseases because they do not or did not forgive their offenders.

I prayed for my offenders and their salvation, and God forgave me. Praying for my offenders is not hard anymore because I want to be free. When you live for vengeance, you are bound or tied up. When you are tied up, you are limited and restricted. In essence, who is being hurt? Your offender or you? Just some food for thought. I believe this prayer will free you from the bondage and begin the forgiveness process:

~Forgiveness Prayer~

> Father, in the name of Jesus, I pray for those who have wronged me, wounded me, treated me badly, said unkind words, persecuted me, hurt me, attacked me with words, mistreated me, beat me down, beat me up, abandoned me, deceived me, manipulated me, let me down, lied about me, lied to me, deserted me, attacked me without cause. I pray that their sins be forgiven them. I pray that they are blessed mentally, spiritually, emotionally, financially, and physically. I pray that their homes are blessed. I pray their jobs are blessed. I pray their family be blessed. I pray for their protection. I pray that they are blessed. I pray that skilled, spiritual laborers will cross their paths and witness the good news, the gospel of Jesus Christ, and that they receive Christ as their lord and savior in the name of Jesus and the power of his blood. Amen.

I pray this prayer every night. Sometime I pray it on demand because I do not want lack of forgiveness to drop its little seedlings. I make it a habit to pray for my offenders all day every day. It has brought peace. It has brought love and forgiveness genuinely and quickly. It has blessed me tremendously. I have received favor, healing, insight, guidance, and, most of all, fellowship with people. God loves people. News flash! God loves everybody, even the unlovable. Even the ones who can be a little "special" at times. Before I got saved, I was not all that lovable, and yet he loved me in my wretched state of being. Wow! Talk about unconditional love!

CHAPTER 8

A Work in Progress

For I know the thoughts and plans that I have for you, says
the Lord, thoughts and plans for welfare and peace and
not for evil, to give you hope in your final outcome.

—Jeremiah 29:11

UPON COMPLETING MY master's degree in social work, I went into the field of human services, working with victims of sexual abuse, domestic violence, traumatic loss, HIV and AIDS, incarcerated women reentering society, and women with developmental disabilities. My heart is there for women suffering mentally, spiritually, emotionally, and physically. When there is hurt, I offer hope through self-exploration and examination. The change process involves the willingness to do the work involved in the transformation. The transformation is a process of taking the steps, making the needed changes, and having the determination to do so.

I am still a work in progress. Life continues to throw me curveballs, but I am learning to be fast on my feet. I still have peaks and valleys, but I do not stay in the valley long. I may have a good cry and continue on my path walking toward the light at the end of the tunnel. I continue to walk through, and I come out on the other side a stronger and wiser person. I still have hills to climb, but victory is sweet when I reach the top of the summit. I have shed many tears, but joy always comes in the morning. I aim to take better care of myself. As a work in progress, I am in a state of continual learning:

- I am learning to love myself unconditionally.
- I am learning not to settle and compromise myself for the sake of others.
- I am learning to let go when people walk away.
- I am learning to cherish and embrace those who have stayed.
- I am learning to listen to my inner voice.
- I am learning to embrace spending time alone with me, myself, and I.
- I am learning only God can love me unconditionally.
- I am learning to look at myself the first thing in the morning—with sleep in my eyes, before brushing my teeth—and mouth the words, "Hello, gorgeous."
- I am learning to give big bear hugs.
- I am learning how to accept a compliment.
- I am learning to smile even when people do not smile back.
- I am learning to give a soft answer.
- I am learning to walk in love even when people hurt or slight me.
- I am learning that patience is a virtue: wait for the Lord.
- I am learning not to take life for granted because tomorrow is not promised.
- I am learning not to take people for granted because situations and circumstances can change quickly.
- I am learning to laugh at my mistakes.
- I am learning that it is okay to disagree.
- I am learning to communicate my wants and needs.
- I am learning to say "no".
- I am learning to strike up a conversation with a complete stranger and enjoy our conversation.

- I am learning to discern the needs of people.
- I am learning that a soft answer turns away wrath.
- I am learning to forgive quickly but to let trust take a while to develop.
- I am learning that I will make mistakes and bad judgments, but will I pick myself up, ask for forgiveness, and re-strategize.
- I am learning that the importance of rest, resolve, and restoration is an ongoing process.

Painful memories of my past will try to present themselves. However, when the enemy tries to mail a special delivery marked "memories of my past," I tell him I am *not* signing for that package.

You may be at a crossroad in your life. You may be lying alongside the pool of Bethesda, waiting for someone or something to make life happen for you, year after year, when you have everything inside of you to start things in motion. You can do it! You may think you are too old or too tired or you waited until it was too late to start over or finish what you started in life. You aren't. You haven't.

As I mentioned earlier, John 5 verses 2-9 talks about a certain man who lay by a pool with an infirmity for 38 years. The Amplified Bible states this certain man suffered deep-seated issues and lingering disorder for 38 years. At the appointed season, an angel would come by and trouble the water, and whoever jumped in would be healed. But the man never jumped.

Well, that angel is troubling the water for you now. Jesus hung on the cross for our sickness and disease 2000 years ago. You are healed. Stop—you don't have to wait anymore for someone to do the work for you! If you want to be whole, you are, if you believe and start the process. I am a true testament that you can do anything you set your heart and mind to do. Your heart's desire may be to go back to school; launch a program or project; start a business; open a day-care center; bake cakes to sell; make scented candles and soaps; become a seamstress; showcase your God-given vocal talent, artistry, or poetic gifts; or write a groundbreaking book or movie. Whatever your desire is, God has already equipped you to succeed. All you have to do is get up and walk in your victory.

Perhaps you have not given your life to Christ. My mental, physical, and emotional healing began that cold morning in December of 1993 when I accepted Jesus as my Savior. I was adopted into the Royal Family with the promise of Eternal Life with Christ. You too can be adopted into the Royal Family with Jesus! Heaven rejoices over one soul. Heaven is happy that you said, "Yes!"

Pray This Prayer:

> Dear Jesus, I am a sinner. I believe that you died and rose from the dead to save me from my sins. I want to be with you in heaven forever. Jesus, forgive me all of my sins that I have committed against you. I here and now open my heart to you and ask you to come into my heart and life and be my personal Lord and Savior. Amen

Welcome to the Family! The next step is to join a Bible-teaching and -believing church to learn of the goodness of Jesus!

CHAPTER 9

From Ordinary to Extraordinary

THAT'S RIGHT! COME out from the mold of ordinary and endeavor to be extraordinary. Tap into your remarkable God-given gifts and talents. In her book, *The Remarkable Women of the Bible*, Elizabeth George states, "It has been a longtime practice of artists to paint over their less impressive works." That is how God is; he had the masterpiece of who we would be in his mind, but it is our free will, our choices, and our behaviors that can delay the masterpiece that God has in mind. If we let him, God will do an extreme makeover in us, and we will be pleased with the outcome.

Allow God to create a grand masterpiece on a canvas that once held a less-than-remarkable picture. You are a grand masterpiece! Underneath the emotional pain of your childhood, abusive relationships, abandonment, rejection, disappointments, setbacks, and dark nights is a divine work of art.

During my masterpiece transition, outwardly I believed I was not good enough, pretty enough, and skinny enough in the sight of man. I allowed people to dictate what was best for me. I was miserable, always trying to reinvent myself: going on crash diets, cutting my hair, growing my hair, coloring my hair, mirroring myself based on people's opinions of me. It never worked! Never! I was miserable, depressed, and angry trying to fit in when I was born to stand out! I was a square peg trying to fit into a triangle. You waste a lot of time and generate a lot of negative energy trying to please someone who doesn't want you in their life because they are a rectangle and you are triangle.

My calling was to assist individuals experiencing the pain and loss I experienced as a child. I like to think of it as paying it forward. As a social-work professional, I gained a wealth of experience and knowledge. I have been employed with the Alzheimer's Association, Michigan chapter; Big Brother/Big Sister of Michigan; the Children's Center of Wayne County, Neighborhood Service Organization, and St. John Open Arms.

As a clinician with the Children's Center, I worked in the family-bereavement program as a grief-and-loss counselor. Remember, I shared earlier how my cousin was on the fast track of her career, globe-trotting the world for her job? Guess what? Soon after I accepted my position with the Children's Center, my employer sent me to Seattle, Washington; Miami, Florida; and Atlanta, Georgia, for conferences that lasted a week! Talk about God giving me the desires of my heart! In addition to my role as a grief-and-loss clinician, I developed a training-and-education component for the Center. My love for teaching and my desire to teach never left me. I love to educate and empower! I have developed training materials to train staff and the community at large. I was selected to do a presentation at the National Organization on Victim Assistance (NOVA) in Atlanta, Georgia, in August of 2005. My topic was "The Grief and Loss Support Group: the Group No One Wants to join." In 2006, I hosted my own radio talk show, "Speaking from the Heart," on WDRJ 1440 in Detroit, Michigan. I truly enjoyed the radio broadcast. In 2007, I presented to the women of AT&T in Kansas on healthy self-esteem.

As an advocate for victims of trauma and violence, I have been a mistress of ceremony for candlelight vigils honoring victims of crime and domestic violence.

Over the years, I developed a niche for myself in public speaking. I speak to share my story of triumph over adversity. I am always overjoyed when people approach me after I tell my story and inform me that they are going back to school to become a social worker after hearing my story of triumph after adversity.

Desires of Thine Heart

Now it's your turn to obtain the Desires of Thine Heart. Please use the following pages to put your Hopes, Plans, Goals, Desires, and Dreams into action.

Desires

_____

_____

_____

_____

_____

_____

_____

_____

_____

_____

_____

_____

_____

_____

_____

_____

_____

_____

_____

_____

_____

Plans

Hopes

Dreams/Goals

_____

_____

_____

_____

_____

_____

_____

_____

_____

_____

_____

_____

_____

_____

_____

_____

_____

_____

_____

_____

Dream Big!

Steps I Need to Take to Achieve My Goals

_____

_____

_____

_____

_____

_____

_____

_____

_____

_____

_____

_____

_____

_____

_____

_____

_____

_____

_____

Who Must I Forgive?

_____

_____

_____

_____

_____

_____

_____

_____

_____

_____

_____

_____

_____

_____

_____

_____

_____

_____

_____

_____

_____

REFERENCES

Davis, June Newman. 1985. *Scripture Keys Power Manual.* Scripture Keys Ministries, Inc. 107.

George, Elizabeth. 2003. *The Remarkable Women of the Bible.* 126.

Merriam-Webster's Dictionary and Thesaurus. 2006.

Noah Webster 1828 (2007) Foundation for American Christian Education

FELECIA A. BERRY, LMSW

Felecia earned her bachelor's degree in social work from Marygrove College and her master's degree in social work from Wayne State University, graduating with honors. As an undergraduate student intern, Felecia implemented the Hamtramck Harvest, a food program for the needy, in the city of Hamtramck. The program is still in operation today.

As a social-work professional, Felecia' has worked for the Alzheimer's Association, Big Brother/Big Sister, My Sister's Place, the Children's Center, Neighborhood Services Organization, and St. John Open Arms. She has provided clinical interventions and treatment to a diverse population of individuals, families, and groups affected by trauma such as sexual abuse, domestic violence, rape, emotional abuse, verbal abuse, suicide ideations/attempts, and grief and loss.

She has volunteered to help women reentering society from the prison system and women with HIV and AIDS.

Professionally, Felecia implemented a training and education component to increase awareness and advocate on behalf of her client population in the community. Felecia has provided trainings at conferences and in schools, churches, and community mental health agencies.

In August 2005, Felecia presented at the National Organization for Victim Assistance (NOVA) in Atlanta, Georgia. Her topic was "The Grief and Loss Support Group: the Group No One Wants to join." In 2007, Felecia presented a workshop for the women of AT&T in Kansas on building healthy self-esteem. In 2007, Felecia presented at an educators' conference at Marygrove College. Her conference topic, on behalf of grieving children, was "Bridging the Gap between Educators and Grief Counselors".

An advocate for victims of crime and trauma, Felecia has been mistress of ceremonies for candlelight vigils honoring victims and survivors of trauma and crime.

In 2006, Felecia hosted "Speaking from the Heart" on WDRJ radio in Detroit. "Speaking from the Heart" provided encouragement based on biblical principles to inspire radio listeners.

If you would like to book Ms. Berry for a workshop, conference, retreat, or speaking engagement, you may email her at FBerry4808@aol.com.

Mailing address:
PO Box 250308
Franklin, Michigan 48025

CPSIA information can be obtained at www.ICGtesting.com
Printed in the USA
BVOW081314081112

305044BV00002B/109/P